HOW TO DEAL WITH A DUMBASS:

What to do and say when they come your way

Lonnee Rey

ThrivingBestSellers.com

I dedicate this book to my longtime friend, Sir John Wallace. He refuses to suffer fools lightly, makes no bones about it, is frequently kicked off FaceBook for calling people out on their lies and posting the facts as he sees them. At age 83, he just doesn't care what "fact checkers" have to say, and laughs, "I'm in FaceBook jail, again!"

Retired US Coast Guard, John has been a confidante and lifesaver to the men in his unit back then, and those he cavorts with to this day. He is a giver and supporter of great causes, including Toys for Tots, where we met a dozen years ago.

Yes, John R. Wallace is a stand-up guy. He represents the kind of person you want to have in a foxhole with you.

CONTENTS

THERE ARE 3 KINDS OF PEOPLE:
The *one* that learns by reading.
The *few* who learn by observation.

And the rest who have to pee on the electric fence for themselves.

PROLOGUE

Have you ever negotiated with your higher power? You know those times when you ignored the 'nudges' and got into hot water? Mine always went something like this:

"OH God, please get me out of this mess alive, and PS - it'd be great if my own dumbass mistakes help someone else someday. All this chaos can't possibly be for nothing. Show me how I can make all of this matter! Show me how I can help others."

Here is how it manifested:

The Craigslist ad read, "Nationally-syndicated talk show looking for guests for special episode on personal safety. Tell us why you need an HIV test and why you haven't done it, yet. If we pick your story we will fly you out to L.A. and..."

My email: **"Dear Producers - I thought we were in love. After meeting in a homeless shelter, we moved in together. I always believed two people could 'come up' stronger together and wouldn't that make a great story someday.**

I had high hopes. He, on the other hand, was out getting high. "Psst. Hey, Miss Lady, your man was sharing needles with some dude." Word from the street. 'OH, OK.' I might have a roof over my head, (good decision), but "unprotected sex with a needle-sharing liar" wasn't so great.

I've been too scared to get an HIV test. If you pick me, know that I have worked in film and television quite a bit and yes, I'd be willing to do a live HIV test with your talk show host.

Hoping to hear back from you,

Signed,

Should Know Better By Now (but clearly do not)"

I was excited for some odd reason, like I knew they would call.

This is what I call "The BIG Yes!" It can look crazy to other people; defy logic, even. But so what? It is what *you* are called to do and that is all that matters. It is your path, after all. Apparently, this was mine. As strange as this might sound to you right now, it all felt so right.

The phone call: "Hello, ma'am. I am a producer at the Tyra Banks Show. 'Sounds like you've got quite the story and reason to get an HIV test. You could inspire millions to avoid the same mistakes. If you're still interested, we would love to have you on a special show dedicated to personal safety."

Well, hell's bells, why not? Television is an effective way to 'hit' a ton of people. I was in. It ended well: all of us were negative. Tyra thanked me for being brave. I was shocked. Brave? Me? I'm nothing more than a dumbass who lived to tell about it.

At that time, I really had no clue how 'off' my judgment was - how gullible I'd been with that guy - how insanely trusting I'd been with the wrong people for quite some time. Clearly, I had poor discernment skills.

Plus, I was desperate to be liked, loved and accepted by anyone. As a result, I was willing to accept everyone. Pretty much anyone who would look my way was automatically on the team; given full trust without exception. It was also enough rope to hang themselves. However, (and maybe you can relate?), they were also given far too many chances to run over my foot, back-up, do it again, and then 'drive away' while I made excuses for their behavior.

Allowing people 'in' that do not belong 'in' gets expensive: the toll on your emotions, self-confidence, physical well-being, friends, friendships and happiness is immense. Therapy bills skyrocket, too, just quietly. It can rob you of motivation, crush your dreams, and derail you with ongoing interruptions. How creative or excited can you be when distractions come in fast and hard? How can you hear your intuition's whispers and follow your inner GPS? If you doubt yourself you simply cannot benefit from this innate guide, can you?

Boy, you sure know how to pick 'em

I have made a ton of bad choices backed with prayer, "*Please make this work out.*" It was wishful thinking: negotiating with God won't get you orange juice from a cow. I have been a total dumbass so I know what it looks like. Thanks to the 'School of Hard Knocks,' I can show you the ropes now. I want to help you choose better.

If you see yourself in these pages, don't worry - "*awareness*" is how your world will morph from caterpillar to butterfly, too.

"Anything more than the truth would be too much."
- Robert Frost, American Poet

Light travels faster than sound.

This is why some people appear bright until they open their mouths.

OLDER AIN'T WISER

It was graduation time. Naturally, I'd been soul-searching for what I *really* wanted to do with my life. In spite of the culinary arts training, it sure as heck wasn't working in food service. I always knew that but Pops insisted on the cooking degree. He was buying. I had no choice. Sigh. Parents will push you into their lane, won't they? My father was a stranger to me. How does someone who doesn't truly know you decide what is right for you to do anyway? Just sayin~

My dream was to travel, have cool adventures, and contribute to world peace. That year, John Denver's concert in the park gave me the spark - the YES - I'd been seeking. I decided that going to work for global peace at his Windstar Foundation in Snowmass, CO, was the next move.

Receiving Snowmass newspapers with headlines like, "Fire Engine Gets New Bell" had me convinced: this was my 'Little House on the Prairie Lifestyle' dream-come-true. I would have pushed a broom just to be there.

Excitedly, I announced it to my staff: "Hey guys, I am so excited!! I got my one-way ticket to Colorado today! I've always wanted to live in the mountains, and I'm going to find work at John Denver's Windstar Foundation." The room fell silent. I expected smiles, at least.

This is the God's honest truth…here is what they said:

1. You can't do that, *you'll die!*
2. You don't have a job yet…*you'll die!*
3. You've never been there before - are you *crazy*??
4. What about your family? How can you leave them… *you will die!*

At that time, I didn't know how to recognize the limited capacity of others to even conceptualize life outside of their own little bubble. While they may have meant well…sheesh. You'd have thought I was going parachuting without the parachute.

Who knew?
After throwing away my airplane ticket, I got a glimpse into the reasons for their responses. None of them had ever left the state of Rhode Island, except for one whose honeymoon was in Boston, an hour away. She came home early because she missed her family too much. Wow.

I was respecting my elders. You know the drill. Just because they were older, I thought they were wiser. They probably thought so, too, just quietly.

Though they projected "what the hell is wrong with you??" with a vengeance, it wasn't *me*. It was limited perspective-having, fear-based 'children' with older faces.

THE LESSON: If you want to hike the Andes, share your dream with hikers not homebodies.

IT ISN'T "WHAT'S WRONG WITH YOU?"

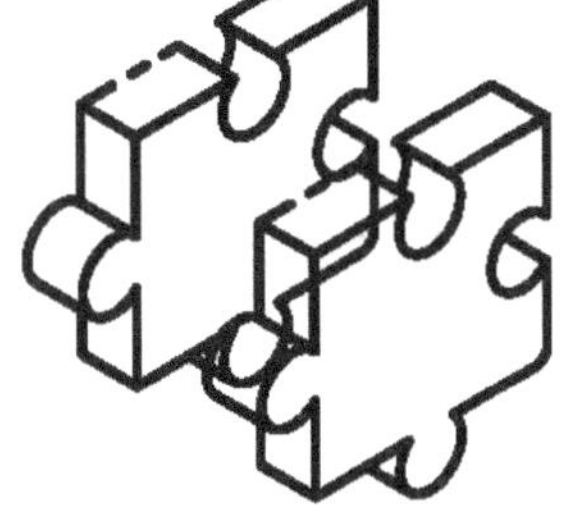

IT'S

"WHO IS WRONG WITH YOU?"

DUMBASS, DEFINED:

dumb·ass

Noun - a stupid person; used to express a low opinion of someone's intelligence.

SYNONYMS:

blockhead, bonehead, dunce, dunderhead, fuckhead, hammerhead, knucklehead, loggerhead, lunkhead, muttonhead, numskull, shithead, dolt, dullard, pillock, poor fish, *pudden-head*, pudding head, stupe, stupid

TheFreeDictionary.com/dumbass

INTRODUCTION

*When you change the way
you look at things, the
things you look at change.*

This book could have been titled, "How to recognize trouble *before* it becomes your problem." It was written so you could stay in the highest state possible when a dumbass crosses your path. It's really about choosing better crew that are in favor of Team YOU. Not everyone belongs in a foxhole with you.

It is pretty simple, really: Let people be who they are *then* decide if they are what you want more of in your life. The way to sidestep extra stupid stuff is to recognize who, exactly, has the potential of laying 'extra stupid stuff' at your feet. All you are doing is *observing what is, for what it is.*

Each of us is dealing with some form of stupid, be it locally, or on the global stage. It is what it is and *it is what it ain't.* I know it's tempting to autopilot a 'knee-the-jerk reaction' but that does not help *you* in the long run. While it might be well-deserved, the truth is this response diminishes your light, lowers your vibration and creates more hot messes *you* have to clean-up.

"How to Deal with a Dumbass" casts light, and light-hearted

humor, on those 'human speed bumps' in life. Look, it's one thing to go bumpity-bump over a hump; it is quite another to continue traveling down that same road, never questioning the path at all.

You may have stumbled one too many times and lost your sense of self along the way. It's OK. Sure, it sucks. But you can bounce back. You've made it this far and the next chapter isn't written in stone. Having skills to deal with a dumbass is empowering, enlightening and exciting!

Imagine being ready for a curveball, or being able to quickly decide what, and *who,* is good for you - right on the spot. Imagine the agility of ducking 'Chinese throwing stars' or avoiding future chaos. That's what this is about.

This is not about being judgmental! This is a book designed to help you use good judgment with compassion. Yes, lots of compassion. There is value in everyone, even the *dim*-asses.

Picking a good team

Collaborations with the right people are really productive - there is exponential power in numbers. I know there is hesitation and fear of getting it wrong again. Grow past these worries so they don't become your future. Just a 1% change lands you somewhere else.

Here are ways to see the signs *before* they smack you in the head. It is like having a superpower to see around corners. Imagine that for a second: it is a *huge* advantage. But in case you are dealing with a dumbass right now, this book offers words and ways to recognize and break free from said dumbass, and never look back. You just need to know how to read the warning signs.

CAUTION: LOW OVERHANG

y cousin, the truck driver, didn't see the signs. You know how they post a few warnings in advance of an overhang? He must have missed a lot of signs. Can you imagine the sound of a roof being sheared off an 18-wheeler?! Whoa. What a dumbass. Would you hire him to drive your truck? Hell to the no! The same is true about a few types of people: letting them back in the door is a (repeat) recipe for more drama, disappointments and discouraging results. You deserve better.

Do not buy into that load of B.S. that says you are supposed to suffer fools, that life is just like that and there is nothing you can do about it.

Tolerating other people's stuff adds weight to your world. It clutters your mind, influences your decisions, and can cause you to make some truly bad choices. You are not required to be an order follower, either. Taking on the dictates of another's agenda, without questioning it first, is like choosing to walk through life with a blindfold. You will have better luck pulling on a wishbone and hoping it works out in your favor.

Identifying the 'load' means you can shake it off. "It" means the guilt trips, the whining, the nagging, and yes, the ridicule cast at you for not being like them: compliant without query.

You question authority before following orders, don't you? You'd better, because there is a global epidemic of non-thinking compliant-driven people whose only reward in life is walking in step with the masses even if it makes no sense whatsoever.

The truth is not offensive, so don't shoot the messenger.

By recognizing weak-links in your world, you leave room for those who, like you, value integrity...and are actively seeking to build a network of trustworthy souls. These are "stand-up guys" that you want in a foxhole with you.

It's time to shrug off the excess weight, y'all.

Who do *you* say YES to?

“Choose your leaders
with wisdom and forethought.
To be led by a coward
is to be controlled
by all that the coward fears.
To be led by a fool
is to be led
by the opportunists
who control the fool.
To be led by a thief
is to offer up
your most precious treasures
to be stolen.
To be led by a liar
is to ask
to be told lies.
To be led by a tyrant
is to sell yourself
and those you love
into slavery.”
-Octavia E. Butler, Parable of the Talents

JACK AND JILL LOVE THAT HILL

Jack is a really charismatic guy. Intelligent and funny, I thought he was a cool dude. However, when his girlfriend stayed with me, the bigger picture wasn't so attractive:

Jack stole his neighbor's car and his plan was to blame it on Jill. What a dumbass. Apparently the 'shots fired' recently near their home was because of it. *They were warning shots,* he told me. You bet they were...*for me.* Duly noted.

Allegedly, 'car theft' was his latest move - a step up from taking car keys off beach blankets and stealing whatever was in that person's car. What a dumbass. It made me glad I never gave him my phone number or address. (Trust your gut, y'all.)

Gotta run, Hon
So, he's a dumbass, huh? I had to decide a few things real quick: was it true? Will I ever go back and hang out like we used to? It was always so much fun. Wait, hold up: how is 'hanging out again' even an option? I trusted Jill more than Jack. Even if only part of it was true, what was I, a dumbass? Duh. But it's true: I *did* wonder about those things for a milli-second. God only knows when the next 'warning shots' would come. This was a warning sign for *me:* stay the hell away from potential potholes and the people who dig them.

Jill was at my house because she feared for her life. I saw the bruises and put ice on her neck. This was serious. I believed she was serious about moving on, as well. Finding her shelter was no easy task because she refused to file a police report. "It will make things worse." Maybe so. She blew-off the only local shelter offering her a room. "I just need to be alone - camp in the woods by myself for a while." She was headed back to Jack's and we both knew it.

This was her pattern, she said. It wasn't easy but I had to draw the line, "Don't ever come to my house, Jill. I care about you more than you care about yourself. Going back for more of the same is your path."

"I know, I'm stuck on stupid."

Yah, but I'm not. I'm *done*.

> **PRO TIP:** If you know someone like Jill, you can try to help but don't be attached to the outcome. Once you see the bigger picture, make a solid decision in your favor. Weigh the pro's and con's on paper if it helps. Then decide: Do *you* want *more* or *less* of people like this in your life? You can see what's coming...the writing is on the wall, after all.

"What we sometimes fail to realize is that with every single one of our Yeses and/or Noes, we are showing others how they are meant to treat us. When we tolerate or excuse behaviors that are disrespectful, insensitive, demeaning, or even dangerous, we are telling the other party that we believe that they have our permission to continue with the words, actions or behaviors they have exhibited."

- Author Paula Alphonse

SPOTTING AT A DISTANCE: THE FIVE RED FLAGS

 **5 Red Flags**

These personality traits are RED FLAGS - people who cannot be trusted to have your back and will probably get in your way along the path.

Pay attention when you see someone acting one of these ways.

They are broadcasting how they will treat you.

Recognize the signs. These 5 Red Flags include:

Be A.W.A.R.E. of those who exhibit one, some, or all of these traits that will trip you up:

- **A**sleep at the wheel - not paying attention; lost in their own little world.

- **W**eak-willed - namby-pamby; lacking courage; "spineless wonder."

- **A**pathetic - "couldn't care less" who they hurt in their path.

- **R**epeat offenders - these people are the definition of insanity.

- **E**rratic - someone you really can't count on.

RED FLAG #1

Asleep at the Wheel

You can lead a horse to water... but you can't make him THINK!

Not the sharpest knife in the drawer

Zzzzz. Asleep at the Wheel folks are a danger to themselves and others. They are not ideal for your team if only because they lack situational awareness. They also make some pretty poor choices. And that's fine for them. Live and let live. All you are going to do, from now on, is observe and remain neutral. In effect, you are not affected. You are in the audience, watching the show instead of playing a lead role in the show. Neutral observer mode will help you enjoy the 'show.' However, if you are seated next to the equivalent of a cymbal-clanging monkey, it can be hard to hear the next line. Time to change seats because they will never change their tune.

Shhhh!

I've done this *hundreds* of times, but the other morning I poured boiling water into the *wrong* part of the coffee press. What's worse is that it took far too long to figure out the problem. DUH. I was Asleep at the Wheel, big time. I was too sleepy to make coffee to wake up. It was one of those days where I should have made instant coffee so I could wake up and make French press coffee. We all have those moments where we think we are present and we are not. Some days we trip or bang into stuff. It's a temporary condition. But some folks insist on 'sleeping' as a way of life. I have learned it is better to avoid than try to awaken them.

I'll never forget this day. I mean, who says this? "I go one step forward and eight backward, Lonnee! I just don't get it. I mean, I know I'm sorta contributing to it all, but still…"

Over the years I'd tried to encourage my neighbor Kristin to realize that her present reality was from planting yesterday's seeds - that she could make a whole new 'crop' if she planted new seeds. "Kristin, you have made some good decisions in the past. You can do it again." This time, my words *really* pissed her off. She slammed her fist on the banister and yelled, "God. Made. Me. A. Dumbass! That is who I am! I AM A DUMBASS!" Whoa.

"OH, OK, then." "Acceptance" is the key to peace. The writing wasn't just on the wall it was broadcasted for the entire neighborhood's benefit. Bonafide Dumbass Alert: steer clear, people.

Trying to lift up a person who wants to stay down is exhausting. It is like pulling a burro uphill: it pisses them off and wears you out. Let people be who they are and often, *where* they are, as-is. Somehow they made it this far in life.

Get in the habit of saying "OH, OK" and then asking yourself, "do I want *more* or *less* of this?" You immediately stop second-guessing your next move and 'ease on down the road.'

Their 'bumper car approach' to life can really wreak havoc in the lives of others. The following story, like all the others you will read, is true. Thank goodness *this* didn't happen at 70 MPH on a main highway:

I thought the wheel was wobbly but...

maybe it's just me?

Kristin said her car was really shaky on the highway. She pulled over, gave it a visual, saw nothing and drove her wobbly vehicle back home.

"I got a call for just one more delivery with Door Dash," she told me. Knowing her, she'd already been drinking when this call came in, but I digress.

Literally 20 yards from home, her front wheel came flying off, bounced across the street, annihilated the neighbor's lawn gnomes and landed squarely in the neighbor's lap. He literally handed her back that tire.

Why do I share this? Imagine that person you know to be flaky, or asleep at the wheel in life. Think twice before you trust their judgement, OK? Imagine what could have happened if she'd been speeding the down the highway with YOU?!

Call the police!
(so I did)

I woke up at 3am for some reason. Half an hour later, six gunshots were fired outside my building. I could hear two men yelling, "I'm gonna *kill you!*" and, "You *shot me, man!*"

The police came, but only one man was caught, hand-cuffed, and in the patrol car. I wondered what happened to the guy who yelled "call the police!"

For all anyone knew, the second suspect was long gone. But noooo...

All of a sudden he appeared from the woods, marched right up to the arresting officers, hurling racial insults the whole way.

I watched them ask him a few questions, then take him down. In about 30 seconds, he was face-down on the pavement, cuffed and *still* swearing.

Can you believe that dumbass came back??

This guy has friends and family, too. No doubt that night was not the first time his sister, who left the scene and returned with him later to find the gun he tossed in some bushes, had seen him act a fool many times already. This type of thing does not just happen, you know?

For all we know, he bragged to friends about the shootout and 'no jail time' - he got away with it, in effect, because no one was injured...just drunk.

LISTEN to what is happening in the lives of others. DECIDE if this what you want in your life because eventually it will weave its way onto your path.

RED FLAG #2

Weak-willed

The 'go along to get along' types who could never have your back because they themselves are lacking 'spine.'

Weak-willed

Easily swayed.
SPINELESS. LEMMING. Words relating to this: cowardly, gutless, soft, spineless, timid, weak-minded, weak-kneed.
Lacking strength of will.

CASE STUDY: Stubborn is Code for Weak

At what age does one lose their voice? Children speak their minds quite freely, but something mysterious happens along the way: invisible duct tape. Whatever the reason, far too many people have lost their free-thinking minds and their mouth has followed suit. Seriously. When did 'what *everybody else thinks* is right, is the right thing to do' become the thing to do?

Since thoughts drive actions, those afflicted with 'laryngitis' also become weak-willed, caving into the 'group think' mindset for no valid reason other than needing to 'belong.' Stubbornly defending their choices, their 'bravado' of strength is quite the opposite.

This chapter covers several ways "weak-willed" undermines the right thing to do. Be it a lack of courage or the alleged 'power' of being stubborn, the result is still the same.

Oh, do tell

I have, no, I *had* a friend who proved to be weak-willed but did his best to couch it as a strength. I must admit I 'bought it' at first. I 'allowed' it for a couple years. But when time came for the 'rubber to hit the road' he always developed a yellow streak down his back. There was more time spent fabricating excuses than anything, really.

He disguised it saying, quite pridefully, "I'm stubborn." As if "stubborn" were a sign of strength. Have you ever been told you're stubborn? It isn't a compliment. It shows limited interest in learning or doing anything new - it is an old dog that refuses to learn new tricks; the sign of a closed mind. Being set in one's ways is fine, but when it comes to the picking, or kicking off the team time, know what they bring to the table. It might work for you, it might not.

Side bar: the opposite of stubborn includes "altruistic" and "unselfish" according to definition. Here is how it shows up:

(cut to a living room chat with this neighbor)

"Nobody's gonna tell me what to do. I'm sure as hell not going to interfere by saying something to someone else. Besides, they won't care anyway." I guess he owned a crystal ball.

This man held his tongue where his speaking up could have saved lives. Yes, it was that serious. No matter how much I begged him to speak up, to save his family and friends from making uninformed decisions, (he said he would); he never did. There was always an excuse like, "I got home late from work" or "I forgot."

Still, I persisted, urging him to share the research I'd given him; research he personally used to make an informed decision. If he knew something like that, and didn't tell me, I'd mad AF at him!!

"Nah, I ain't sayin' a thing. I don't need them getting mad at me." THERE it was, plain as day: it was about *him.* His reputation was more important than anything. 'What other people think disease' was in full bloom. Can you see how this is a coward appearing to be principled? It is not "strength." Hardly a "stand up guy."

> **INSIGHT:** We have all been weak, said 'yes' when it was 'no.' None of us is perfect at 100% authentic responses. However, if you see it in someone and it's the majority of their 'style,' the writing is on the wall: s/he will let you down because their 'image' is their primary concern.

Are those hot pants?

I started to notice this "stubborn streak" one sunny day in particular: He was invited to join me at the quarry for a lakeside breakfast cookout. Told to wear sandals and shorts to suit the

90+ degree weather, he showed up in polyester dress slacks, a long-sleeve polyester zip-up black shirt, and lugs.

I suggested he change to be comfortable and he snarled, "If I go back in my house I'm not coming out. I am not changing. Nobody's telling me what to do. Let's go."

"Are you sure? Look, if this isn't a "BIG Yes!" for you to do this today, that's OK. I will go alone, no problem." I tried to give him an easy-out.

"I got my shorts on underneath these pants. Let's go. I said I would do this so let's just go do this."

Snappish. Ya reckon I hit a nerve?

Breakfast was 'chill,' but as the morning heat index rose past 90, I could see him sweating balls. "Since you have shorts on, why not wade into the water, man?"

He declined. I'm sure you can do the math: he was lying about the shorts.

Eventually he said, "I should have listened to you, changed clothes and put on sandals."

Uh-huh. But ya get 5-stars for being stubborn.

This single incident is an indication of bigger issues. Do you think I care what his issues are? I did. I used to. I tried to reason with him on many occasions. He would smile and nod like he was listening, then ask me about the very thing I'd just spoken of.

Once, he said he would return to help me with a roadside yard sale, and he never came back. I had to whizz, but couldn't leave my stuff. Do you think this is someone you can count on to have your back? The small stuff tells you so much about a person. While he may have survived into his 60s, it does not make him a wise man. Age *is* just a number.

I once had a boss who was just the nicest gal you'd ever want to meet. Over the years I heard, "I don't like confrontation" a lot. Watch out when you hear that phrase! It is the first sign s/he will not be a "stand up guy" if you ever need them to be. They will not have your back, ever.

The long-and-short of this story is that she did not back up her cleaning crew. We texted pictures of how bad the black mold was and why we refused to touch it. "Well, the maintenance man said it was just dirty," she said. But, but, but we told you how disgusting this is and you listened to *him?* **"I just don't like confrontation.** I told the client I would find somebody to get it done anyway." She willingly endangered all of us, but asking a young gal, nine months pregnant, to remove layers of black mold *really* pissed me off and I stopped the girl from doing it.

At some point, you will encounter this type of super-sweet, laugh at all your jokes, kind-hearted, weak-willed, self-centered person, too. Like "hot pants" who refused to speak up, her main concern was being liked first. It didn't matter the danger posed to us healthy folks, in an apartment that stunk to high-heaven of mold, let alone a young mother about to deliver another baby the next day. This is what apathy looks like.

Both of these people could have, and probably should have, spoken up. Watch what people do, or don't do, as the case may be. They are examples of who to avoid. Mind you, I am not advocating for loud mouths, I'm showing you what a stand-up guy is, and is not.

TEAM BUILDING TIP: Weak-willed, disguised
as "nicey-nice" and 'everybody's friend,' is not
a strong candidate for your foxhole.

when your self-worth
is tied to being
likable...

*you will lower
your standards*

and accept the
unthinkable.

I want to encourage you to be bold in your steps, words and choices. Do what is right *for you.* Indeed, the two people just mentioned were doing what was right for them: fear-based complacency. When reputation or identity is wrapped-up in being liked, weak-willed people will let you drown. I know that sounds cold or harsh, but it is the truth.

If you are called to do something other people don't 'get' don't be surprised. Just note it, considering the source. Remember, we cannot 'give' what we do not possess. Conversely, if a person is fearful or weak, they act out of weakness and fear. It is what they bring to the table.

It can appear to be a concern for your well-being, and maybe it is in some weird way. But, in building your team and moving forward, be aware of the discouragement factor they 'offer' you. It is all they know, after all. And that's OK. They just don't belong on your team. What you want is a stand-up guy.

Given that 'like attracts like,' it behooves all of us to transmute our own tendency to be weak-willed *if only to draw to us it's opposite*: people who are **bold**. By definition, bold is "not hesitating or fearful in the face of actual or possible danger or rebuff; courageous and daring." These are the people you want on your team. These are the people who will have your back, not abandon you in times of need.

Name one bold move can you make in your life right now. Is it saying 'no' instead of 'yes' next time? Good! Honor how you feel. This one choice will make a huge difference over time. The weak-willed are not strong enough to support you. Eventually, they will be the reason you fall or experience devastating disappointment, *again.*

Finding your way, *doing it your way*, is an act of boldness, in a way. It scares the crap out of these people, too. Is there any other way to live a full life, though? Think of things you have always wanted to do and how it would feel if tomorrow were suddenly your last day - would you be glad you held back? Would you be happy you listened to someone else's ideas for *your* life? Will you live the life you were born to lead, or the one others think is best for you? Some of those "others" are dumbasses. Sorry not sorry. As you will see, handing over your power to another person is a formula for disaster.

Does it seem scary to boldly go where you have not yet gone before? That is perfectly normal. In fact, anything new will be uncomfortable, at first. As a baby, you had an average of 500 falls before standing up and taking a step. Be encouraged by this - you have already triumphed over one of the biggest obstacles of your life: overcoming gravity and fun of crawling around on all fours.

Your "BIG Yes!"

Do the thing that calls to you. So what if it looks crazy to other people or defies logic in their minds? Half of them are nuts anyway, living under a rock or in the shadow of some authority figure who has no right to be there in the first place, but they don't question it. How sad, but again, that is their path, not yours.

Color outside the lines. It's how our greatest inventions have been created: outside "normal" standards. Base it on your "BIG Yes!" not someone else's fears, dictates or hidden agendas. What calls to you is for *you*. No one else was born to walk in your shoes, so don't expect them to tie up your laces and pat you on the back as you brazenly go forth in life.

The Alaskan Adventure

My first job out of culinary school was on a private charter yacht. It appeared that I was finally going to fulfill my dream: a Jimmy Buffet lifestyle, roaming from port-to-port, *free as a bird.*

It turned out that this 92-foot luxury yacht was a floating prison, the captain was known as "The Asshole of the High Seas," and there was me, *the seasick chef.* Our charter guest was a 75 y.o. pervert who pinched my ass, blew cigar smoke in my face, treated me like his personal maid *and* stayed longer than any guest in history: 10 very long weeks. When the captain announced a two-week extension, I jumped ship. A person can only take so much.

Returning to my home state of Florida, I found myself sharing a house and playing 'mom' again to my twin brothers. It was as if my childhood were repeating itself all over again. UGH. Surely life was going to get better, right? Here's the thing: nothing changes unless you do. This was my line in the sand.

Upon hearing a college friend was working on cruise ships in Alaska, I got a serious case of travel envy. Of course, I would skip working cruise ships and find work in a restaurant. That was the plan. I didn't share it with anyone. The projected fears from those Providence, R.I., 'elders' taught me to keep my mouth shut and keep moving.

What few items that didn't sell in my yard sale were packed into an Army duffle bag. I'd seen that on TV, so it must be the way of the traveler, right? Everything I owned was in that bag. Well, 70lb was the airline's weight limit. I'd let go of a *lot.* I figured I would "make it" come hell or high water. "Stuff" can be replaced. Besides, given the 'known,' the unknown was far more appealing.

During the non-stop flight from Daytona Beach to Anchorage,

there was plenty of time to get chummy with the 12 year old seated next to me. She didn't seem to think I was crazy at all.

"What will you do when the plane lands?" she asked.

"I have no idea, yet. All I know is that I have chef's knives and a Summa cum Laude degree from a top-notch cooking school. The rest is up to chance, I reckon."

"Well, my dad's a doctor in Anchorage..."

She paused. I couldn't help wondering where this was going.

"...and we have put people up before. He might be open to having you stay with us."

"Great! Let's go meet your dad!"

It was an immediate 'yes' from him. "Stay for a few nights until you figure out what's next." I was so grateful for his kindness! However, 'something' in me was reluctant to unpack. That 'something' in me felt 'off.'

I hesitantly approached him: "Sir, where do people go when they are traveling?"

"The youth hostel," he replied. "Hostel" was a new word to me but it seemed like 'yes' so I hustled back out the door. They dropped me off at the youth hostel with a wave of 'good luck.'

In line, I noticed a girl from my plane. "Put me in her room, please." I figured she was up to something good.

"Yep. 'Got a summer job at Denali National Park. I'm taking the train up there tomorrow."

Going with her felt like a "BIG Yes!" to me. With my stellar accolades, I figured they'd be glad I showed up - kitchens are *always* short-staffed.

The eight-hour train ride was exciting, though sometimes, it can be hard to know the difference between 'excited' and 'scared.'

I thought back to my childhood, when I first started packing to run away. Twenty-years later I finally did it. No cell phone, no house keys, no bank account; the sense of freedom was indescribable. Yes, this was definitely *exciting.*

Duh-nali

We piled into the small personnel office to sign-in. The possum-faced personnel director glared over her eyeglasses, "You are not on the list. All the jobs are filled. The lodge is full and employee housing is not an option since you don't work here. Maybe you can stop back in two weeks to see if we have had no-shows. N-E-X-T!"

"STOP BACK?! You don't just 'stop back in' at Denali - it's in the middle of nothing, ma'am." She didn't care. I was pushed out of line and given the 'good luck' wave again.

It was a *devastating* blow. How could this have been a "BIG Yes"?? I stood in the corner of that small office with tears streaming down my face. This wasn't excitement; this was fear. I had no clue what to do, the train did not return until morning and I had nowhere to sleep that night. The month of May is still *quite chilly* - almost as cold as that woman in personnel. What was I going to do?

"Hey, I heard what just happened. I saw you on the train ride up here." A young man's voice interrupted the flood gates. "I got my job situated and have a place to sleep in employee housing."

I sobbed out "congratulations" as best as I could.

"No, no, you don't understand. I also brought a tent."

>sniff< "...good..for...you." I tried to sound supportive.

"No, no, *listen:* you can borrow my tent for the night and figure it all out in the morning."

"OMG, thank you! Wow. Really?" I stopped crying long enough to do some math: "Uhm, can you please show me how to put up a tent?" I'd come to Alaska dragging a duffle bag full of books, high heels and CDs, expecting to be working in a kitchen, in a city; not camping in Denali National Park.

In the morning, I met two Aussies who'd been hitchhiking for months. After returning the tent, the three of us set out on the adventure of a lifetime. Our first 'thumbs out' took us the entire way: 135 miles up to Fairbanks. A huge dog in the back of the pick-up truck kept us all warm. It was magical, let me tell ya.

Unfortunately, Fairbanks kinda sucks. I *had* to keep moving. Checking the want ads, I got lucky: "banquet waitress needed!" The job was in Coldfoot; they hired me on the spot, over the phone. "Just get here when you can," they said.

It sounded like a cool job. Sorta. At least it was an adventure! Sure, I had *no idea* where I was going except "north." As if it mattered…I stuck my thumb out again and the first person to come along was a park ranger headed to Coldfoot, 60 miles above the Arctic Circle line. It was an eight hour drive. What are the odds, right? That's what following your BIG yes looks like, my friend.

You may recall "Ice Truckers" on TV? Coldfoot is the dirt truck stop they use. It is also where busloads of people stop for a night to feast on halibut, then attempt to sleep in one of their cardboard hotels with blackout curtains. The full sun of summertime does have its challenges, you know. In the morning, they would pile back into the bus bound for the top of the world: Prudhoe Bay.

Work was easy, albeit boring. I made friends with the Brooks Range pilots and even got to take a helicopter ride on my birthday. Another time, a C-plane pilot took me for a ride, landing right on the river bed. Amazing. Sadly, he crashed his plane two weeks later - downdrafts kill more pilots than anything. I felt sad for him and grateful that I had had good timing.

They say, "when it's your time to go, you go." Maybe that's why I was so brazen (or was it stupid?) announcing: we are going to hike up and waive to y'all from the top of Green Mountain. It looked like a hill from where we stood. *Wrong.*

Amuck-n-Mess
With 22 hours of daylight, navigating by the sun is impossible. We lost our way up that 'hill,' ending up in a field of marsh that quickly turned to tundra. Tundra is like quicksand: one step and you sink...and you keep sinking!

They say "necessity is the mother of invention." We had no idea what to do, but quickly realized that standing at the base of a tree, with roots to stabilize your footing, was the answer. Hang on for dear life, steady yourself, and keep jumping. Every misstep will cause you to sink into tundra and wake up a million mosquitoes sleeping just below the muck. We were covered in mosquitoes, leaping like idiots, and praying for solid ground. We found it, thank God.

Some would have called me a dumbass for trying to hike what looked like a hill. It was not. I didn't know what I didn't know. A "greenhorn" is just plain ignorant. Who knew tundra was going to be our downfall?

We didn't come across a beaver dam on the way in, so this wasn't exactly a good thing to stumble upon - or IN, either. Beaver dams are slick, be it on top or on the sides. That water was cold AF, too. Squishing the whole way back to camp, I vowed to buy waterproof hiking boots if I lived through this hike. The high heels had to be ditched along with the books, CDs and dress clothes. Once treasured possessions, they no longer had value. In fact, they became a burden.

The art of traveling light - letting go of what no longer serves and believing your needs will be met along the way, was *the lesson* of The Alaskan Adventure.

INSIGHT: When you let go your hands are more open to receive; the load you carry is much lighter along the way. Often there is no way to see HOW it will work out, but it *always* does.

All who wander are not lost

It may be uncomfortable, but not knowing your way turns out ok. If you think back to times when you had no idea how to unravel, undo, recover…whatever…you still did it. You managed to make it out and move on. Ask for help along the way, be it literal directions or Divine Intervention.

Back in Anchorage, map in hand, determined to find a hotel, I should have taken a right but took a left. No surprise there. I can get lost in a mall.

Two blocks into being lost, I came across a perpetual yard sale. I mean, it was a Tuesday, so it was sorta weird. Most of the people there had backpacks, and I meandered in to check it out. Maybe it was a sign. Turns-out it was an informal hostel and the backpackers were working the yard sale to earn a spot on the floor for the night.

When in Rome…

By 11am I was making pancakes for 13 people. Having earned my spot on the floor, I headed for downtown on a borrowed bicycle. A really tall guy with a huge backpack was slowly walking down the sidewalk. I'd seen that type of saunter before: it was the walk of someone with no particular schedule. Screeching to a halt next to him, I asked, "What's your deal, dude?" We had a few beers and before I knew it, I was returning the bicycle to tag along with him.

Greg had been traveling under the radar for 14 years. He was a great travel buddy - all the equipment and know-how a "greenhorn" like me needed. Together, we traveled to Seward,

Homer and a few other tourist spots.

Summer was waning and I was anxious to hit Seattle, Vancouver, Vegas, San Diego. I had plans, man. When I said good-bye to Greg, I never expected to run into him again, but I did - literally. Like, literally ran into him on a busy street corner a month or so later.

"I thought I'd find you," he said.

What are the odds? I went to Seattle for three days and ended-up staying for eight years. Plan is a 4-letter word.

The Alaskan Adventure was a series of "BIG Yes!" moments that always worked out. Had I taken a right instead of a left turn that fateful day, map-in-hand, goodness only knows how different the story might have turned out. 'Something' bigger than me knew the way.

"What you want wants you even more than you want it."
-Mark Victor Hansen, co-author, "*Chicken Soup for the Soul*"

When you follow your "BIG Yes!" life will take care of you each step of the way. My taking a huge leap into the unknown might have seemed crazy to others but it turned out to be one of the best things I ever did. It showed me what I want to show you: it *always* works out. Keep following your BIG yeses and you will be astonished how the next step unfolds for you.

If I had listened to those scaredy cat elders in Rhode Island *none* of my life adventures would have happened: riding a camel in Morocco, learning to SCUBA in the Philippines, living in a hut on Maui, exploring crop circles in England, working in Australia, managing BB King, Jr., whom I met coming off a Mississippi River standup paddleboard and remote camping trip, speaking to 400 adventurers at "YEStival" outside of London, being a guest on two national talk shows...the list goes on.

Had I listened to my dad who said, "You can travel when you're older" I would have lived the same life he lived - and he looked miserable. Timing-wise, I would only just be getting started if I'd walked Pop's recommended path 25 years ago.

It takes a strong person to do things nobody else 'gets.' Remember, the weak-willed are never going to be stand-up guys and the stubborn will argue for their ignorance. Closed minds let in no light.

If you notice these traits, know they represent weak links in the chain. Don't be surprised when they are not only unable to support your vision, but might actually try to hold you back.

My dad thought I should be living life his way. But, even when I did life his way and became an entrepreneur with $10k in the bank, he called me a liar. A screenshot of my bank account was given to him; silence was the response. Sometimes, you can never win no matter what you do or say.

Just decide if you want more or less of that treatment and be on your way. Find supportive people who will have your back in hard times. **Accept nothing less.**

TEAM BUILDING TIP: People can only give you what they own. It's OK. You are not bound by law to take it.

RED FLAG #3

Apathetic

Apathetic People Appear Not To Care

But They Do…They Just Don't Care About You.

Apathetic

Not interested; disconnected; don't give a damn; insensitive; callous; cold; showing little concern for others it is *wildly selfish* behavior.

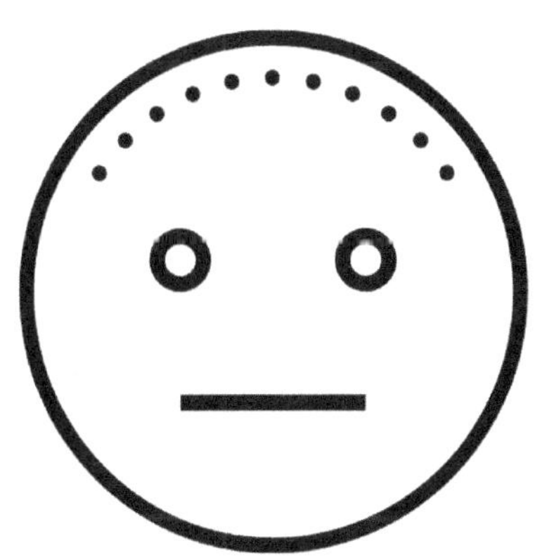

Nothing to Lose

My mother would yell, "Evolve!!" before she squashed a cockroach. I guess that helped one or both of them somehow. Maybe those roaches will thank her personally in the afterlife. I wish she'd had the same consideration when squashing the spirit of a child. People can only give what they are.

Similarily, apathetic people will squash you without yelling "Evolve!!" These are *dangerous* people. Though you might not see the actual cat being swung by its tail, the apathetic are doing just that: metaphorically swinging cats by their tail and not giving a damn who gets clawed. If you see someone losing their mind, acting as if they have nothing (else) to lose, steer clear, Honey Child. Their lack of concern or empathy for their fellow human beings is just the beginning.

Look at the global stage and ask yourself, "Are these 'leaders' *truly* looking out for us?' You can know them by their actions not their words. Note they launched untested experimental drugs on the population. People became human trial experiments. The results are horrifying! Sadly, if you've only watched mainstream television you wouldn't have a clue about the millions of people who have been permanently and severely injured; you wouldn't know the manufacturers have zero liability in the loss of lives; and you would be shocked to learn that a casket maker said "We have gotten 5 years' worth of orders for childrens' coffins in the last 7 months." You can find these truths and terrifying evidences on alternative platforms such as Bitchute, where nurses, doctors and regular folks are screaming at the tops of their lungs about these horrific end results. And yet, these things are still being pushed as "safe and effective." They are not. This is what apathy looks like. Care enough yourself to go find out what is happening because those who are pushing their products to the tune of multi-billions in profits won't care enough to tell you the truth.

Their selfish agendas are cleverly disguised as caring, but if you look a bit deeper, it is a ruse. Would you trust an apathetic person to have your back? IF they do, count it as a one-off. You got lucky. They may be trying to win your trust; sort of how politicians change their tunes in election years, really. Watch what they do when they don't realize you are watching.

If you catch 'em in the act, expect a lie; a cover-up story, at best. Expect others to give shallow-excuse-laden hall passes. Just don't expect an apology. It takes a big person to own-up to their errors.

The unfunny comedy of errors and claims made by authorized personnel is global collusion, the likes of such the world has never seen before, carried out by apathetic 'leaders' who know better, but just don't care.

Discern "hero" from a "zero" and you're golden. *That* is how to deal a dumbass on the global stage.

Smiling Faces
Collaboration takes cooperation. It begins with genuine interest in the 'whole,' not solely that of political stump squad, or local individual commanding the microphone.

They will charm and disarm you, so be careful. One of the best ways to recognize their true nature is conversation: Can you get a word in edgewise? Do you feel heard? Does it seem like they care about you or what you have said? No? Does someone like this currently have a place on your team? FIRE THEM.

Be strong because being weak-willed around this type will hurt you. I know it can be difficult to face-off with someone you love, or are *expected* to respect. You want to be a nice person to everybody, but the truth is, you cannot be friends with everyone.

Will it leave a gap in your world? Yes, thank God. It leaves room for **stand-up guys** to come in because you are no longer dealing with cat-swinging creeps and apathetic imbeciles.

Don't drink poison just because you're thirsty.

Keep your standards high and look for people who are strong enough to encourage you to fly. Look for people who feel authentic, are informed, and walk their talk. Nothing less will do. Be vigilant. Your peace is worth it.

How do you deal with an apathetic person? With some really big ear plugs and a very long walk - the other way. How do you know they apathetic? Because of the way you 'sense' their projected energy at you: if you have to question it, then you have the answer, huh?

If they cut you off, force the conversation into their lane repeatedly, and appear not have heard you, bingo! You know you are dealing with a selfish and apathetic person.

WHEN you notice it, and you will, don't keep giving them a pass, or feel as if you should just "be polite." Their behavior doesn't change. Run the other way. It doesn't mean you have become apathetic; it means you get out of harm's way. *That* is using good judgment!

◆ ◆ ◆

I heard of a recent poll where fans were asked, "Would you steal a pack of cigarettes for your favorite celeb if s/he agreed to sign that pack and send it back to you?" Do I need to tell you the majority said they would do it? I reckon they were counting on a 'get out of jail free' card, eh? smh

Today, celebrities will happily tell you how to live, what to put into your body, to grow caterpillar eyebrows, that twerking looks good - whatever. But WHY? At what point do you think a total stranger is the best person to trust in what's right or true for you?

Actress Nicole Kidman has done a commercial showing how yummy it is to eat a live bug. Oh, isn't she just a great role model to follow? What they aren't telling you is that even the "farmed bugs" are full of dangerous parasites. Kim Kardashian has a similar commercial about near-meat. She looks like a robot, doesn't she? Well-paid *fakes*.

How do you deal with anybody **acting** like they have authority to advise you on matters of health, hope or heart? Regardless of what happens, *no matter what they say:*

1. "Ohhh, OK" is your response, whether out loud or to yourself.
2. Decide if you want *More* or *Less* of their behavior, authority or influence.
3. Move your feet accordingly. (see *5 Ways to Deal with a Dumbass* section)

What is the criteria for your team? Your home team - the one(s) you know will be there in a pinch. Listen to those precious friends - at least they know you enough to advise well. **Trust. It's only everything.**

Have the courage to say 'no thanks.' You can do it by turning off the nightly news readers or the friends who discourage your dreams.

Things are not what they seem, nor are they otherwise.

"Most of the time, we see only what we want to see, or what others tell us to see, instead of really investigating to see what is actually there. We embrace illusions only because we are presented with the illusion that they are embraced by the majority. When in truth, they only become popular because they are pounded at us by the media with such an intensity and high level of repetition that its mere force disguises lies and truths. And like obedient schoolchildren, we do not question their validity and swallow everything up like medicine. Why?

Because since the earliest days of our youth, we have been conditioned to accept that the direction of the herd, and authority anywhere — is always right."

— **Suzy Kassem**, *Rise Up and Salute the Sun: The Writings of Suzy Kassem*

the herd isn't always right, is it?
and now you know what NOT to do

SOCIAL MEDIA

Keyboard warriors and bots abound. Demeaning and inflammatory remarks made from behind the wall of anonymity can be found on nearly every social media platform. Their attempts to discredit are obvious. See it for what it is: gaslighting. Engaging with them is what *they* want you to do. The whole point of this book is making better decisions independent of others, no matter who they are.

It can be tempting to jump in the ring and respond at their base level but don't - it is, in effect, feeding the animals. It is inviting a dumbass to come back to the table and clang their cymbals some more. Keep in mind 'they' may also be bots or trolls paid to diminish the value of a video or posted content. Everytime they post, they get paid. When you respond you are feeding the machine of negativity (and profit), effectively encouraging them to keep doing it. They bit your finger - don't stick it back in the cage.

These 'bandits' rob you of confidence when it comes to speaking your truth. Please know that you are dealing with a dumbass dedicated to destroying, not building up, the community at-large. They aren't worth your time or energy. Keep doing what you do.

I have learned the futility of trying to make sense with the willfully ignorant. They will take pleasure in attacking you and invite others to do the same thing in their cancel culture style. I didn't expect the collateral damage to be so high, but it was.

The attackers erased their comments (unbeknownst to me - I'd moved on), making it appear that I was going off like a nut about something. My social circle of "friends" launched their attack, next. Although they only saw half the posts, they responded 'at' me. It didn't matter that the thread was disjointed, the time stamps were misaligned, etc. - these friends, both local, business and on social media, took what they saw and ran with it. Consequently, I was attacked again, and lost "friends" over it.

The value of a jerk

Sadly, I stood by watching as friends went into a frenzy. Who knew their response would be so callous? Trying to explain myself didn't matter. **Closed minds let in no light.** Willful blindness and willful ignorance appear to be a popular approaches to life, especially when others are enrolled in the plot to belittle someone else.

The gift in this is clear, however: there is value in a jerk. Sucker punches hurt but knowing *who* is throwing the punches is helpful. Sure, it is disappointing to discover but in the end, this is good intel. Learning who would take a string of odd posts, and use it to create *more* commotion, is news you can use. **Delete the need to understand.** People do what they do no matter who you are to them. Remember this very important concept: just because you are close to someone does not mean they won't eventually cast their evil ways upon you. No one is immune.

The times we live in are wrought with deception. Your ability to discern fact from fiction, good people from not-so-good people, is how you can 'surf' the tidal waves of confusion.

Rebounding from it all is the most important skill you can have: agility combined with mobility. "OH, OK!" Dud? Stud? Friend or foe? You have to figure who gets to stay and who has *got* to go: it might be *you.* Lace up those boots, saddle up your horse, and *ride.* It's quicker to check-out than it is to engage or fixate on these keyboard warriors. This isn't paranoia, this is reality.

The best thing you can do is back away - do not feed the animals - don't encourage them by engaging them. Defend your peace with all your might because this has become the norm for today, but it needn't become your theme song:

Birds on a wire set out to conspire and ruin my sunny day.

Their form of jollies is discrediting or maligning truth. Don't allow them to set foot in your head or heart, honey. It isn't worth the therapy bills.

CASE STUDY: STEVE HARVEY

"A lot of people make money off of fear and negativity and any way they can feed it to you is to their benefit in a lot of ways. You can't avoid it completely; you have to be open enough that shit doesn't stick on you, *it goes through,* because you are gonna be hit and bombarded all the time with negativity... You just let things go on through without trying to stop them or block them."
-Willie Nelson

It can be tricky to know who is up to what, frankly. Take Steve Harvey, for instance. Unlike Jerry Springer's show, The Steve Harvey Show appeared to be 'solid.' Harvey positioned himself as an authority figure - a male Oprah, at times, even. Authentic, genuine, caring...the whole shebang. Still, he's an actor, playing a role that serves the viewing audience and makes his sponsors a ton of money.

Harvey is playing a role because viewer ratings fuel the machine. He does it well enough to gain big money contracts with sponsoring companies who also profit from his playing that role. While his intentions as a talk show host and alleged "expert" may be wholesome, he is apathetic to the impact on his guests. I know, I was one of them: played for a fool and used like a tool.

I didn't see it coming. After all, the experience on Tyra's show was nothing but authentic. The show producers genuinely cared about illustrating the ways in which we endanger our own personal safety. I was expecting an authentic show this time, too.

After taping the show that brought me to tears, we had to literally 'corner' Harvey in the hallway just to get a photo. His body guards said, "Steve doesn't do fan pictures." My date, Tedd, was undeterred. You can see by the look on Harvey's face that he was none-too-happy about our photo-op. Maybe he felt bad? (yah, right) He'd pretty much used me, the show was over, and that was all he gave a crap about. Sorry not sorry, that is what happened and "reality."

I had no idea that becoming the featured guest on "The World's First Blind Date Dating Show" was really signing up to be blindsided by a national talk show host. In fact, it wasn't until after that picture was snapped, and we left NBC studios, that my "date" revealed his role in it: they coached him to say nothing. Just smile, sit there and look like a good guy. Let her do all the talking. No one told me this was their agenda all along.

The live audience members boo'd me; viewers bought into the storyline. For months afterward, I was called all sorts of nasty names by friends of my "date."

I thought Steve Harvey was going to do what the 'call' said on his website: "Has it been a long time since you've been on a date? Would you like Steve's help?" I thought he had something real up his sleeve. I was game...I just didn't know I was THE game.

OH, OK. Chock it up to the School of Hard Knocks. Duly noted. Live, learn and *say it forward*.

Have you ever been the brunt of a joke and felt like a total dumbass? This is what happened to me:

I was so excited to be on Steve Harvey's "World's First Blind Date Dating Lab." I later learned they script "reality TV" (which is fine) *but,* don't always tell the guests what they are up to. In fact, I was blind-sided. The entire show was built around a set-up so that Steve Harvey could be "the expert" on my alleged problem. He was nice off-camera and not-so-nice on the show - this set-up was so he could be an "authority" at my expense. I was nearly in tears on the show. Turns out they told my date to be quiet - to say nothing at all no matter what; to let me do all the talking. Steve's "expert advice" was "Ladies let the man talk once in awhile." What a set-up!

Just because you see something on network TV *does not mean it is reality.*

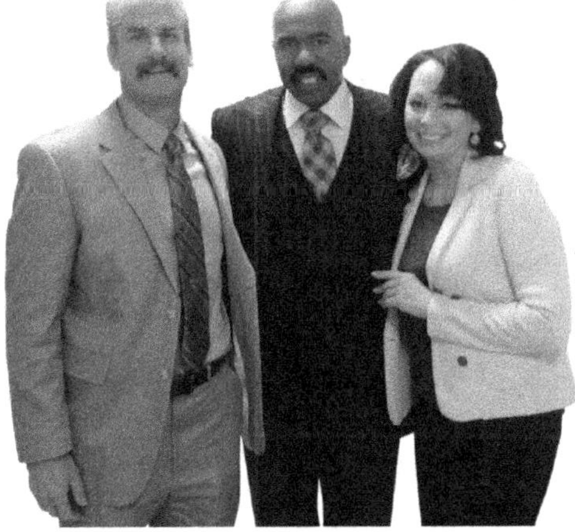

Tedd,
Steve Harvey
&
the author
(30lbs ago)

The actor who played Archie Bunker, Carroll O'Connor, did such a great job on "Archie Bunker" that he was assaulted, rejected by fellow actors, and 'hated on' with humiliating insults while just trying to live his life off-camera.

Actors ACT. News readers read SCRIPTS. Reality TV is loosely based on reality, at best.

Step back a few paces and see the *show* for what it is: like a pro wrestling match with chosen outcomes. Life today is being forced upon us, based on agendas that do not serve the people as much as the profits.

Change the channel: you are in charge of what you tune in to, what you take in, what you believe and how you follow, or not, what's being fed to you. When it comes to the news, understand they are talking heads, not reporters. They are fed the lines according to someone else's agenda. If you doubt this, then go watch real reporters and real news on other platforms and see what you have been missing.

Don't listen to these dumbasses. They have *positioned* themselves as authority figures, but half those on your TV every night aren't even elected officials! Can you imagine what would happen if everyone woke up and just said "NO MORE!"? Imagine the entire world or heck, even 10% of the population, collectively laughing them off stage? The level of lunacy we are witnessing needs to stop. **It can stop with you, today, no longer accepting the force-feeding of bullshit.** Enough already.

RED FLAG #4

REPEAT OFFENDERS

R
Repeat offender

In this case, it's that friend who keeps going back for more of the same.

In spite of poor results, repeat offenders show no obvious intention to alter approach, course or direction.

By far the most exhausting type of dumbass is the REPEAT OFFENDER.

When you find people like this, know one thing: each one of them is dealing with so much of their 'stuff' they've little room to be anything but a burden to you. Again, sorry not sorry. It is what it is, and it is what it ain't.

As a kind-hearted soul, you may have tolerated friends that beg for help but never implement it. Chances are this has gone on for far too long. You need to raise the bar - or get squashed by your low standards of care. Repeat offenders never pick up the clue phone but will certainly be calling you late at night with the same old story.

Once again, this is not about you becoming apathetic to their problems. Only they can surmount their personal issues, of course. The issue is letting them 'in the door' carrying the same burdens as before, S.O.S.: Stuck On Stupid.

Do you want *more* or *less* of this now? Right now. Is this pattern working for you? Are you the people-pleaser type who cannot bear the thought of rejecting someone? Are you the *friend* of someone who can't break old habits? I feel for you. Sometimes, you just need to EXIT as a way of avoiding more of the same from 'them' and running the risk of being a REPEAT OFFENDER yourself.

But I love her...
sometimes love isn't enough

Matt has this thing for troubled women, apparently. And they have it for him. No judgement cast here. If that's what works for some people - that's fine - for them.

As the friend of a "Repeat Offender" though, the 'tax' is pretty high. Maybe you have that friend who calls, cries, swears "it's over" (again) but it isn't?

Matt fell for Erica.
Erica had Matt arrested the first week they started dating.

So, Matt did what any dumbass would do: he married her.

I didn't get to see him again (her wishes) until three years and several arresting 'moments' later, when they finally divorced.

Matt moved on to another 'hot mess.' And I moved on from Matt.

I hated to end a six year friendship with Matt: we'd had so many great times together! And yet, there were many times I did not want to answer the phone when he called. It was bound to be another boo-hoo session, pleas for insights and then repeats of the same patterns. Sticking around, hoping he would magically outgrow his attraction to Jerry Springer-level women wasn't fair to either of us.

It is entirely possible to love someone and not like them one iota. As you know, this book is meant to help you choose who to keep on your team. Distancing yourself from repeat offenders is still allowing them to be who they are, as they are. That is their path, after all.

Recognizing a repeat offender and taking action (yes, that's what's next) is the only way to shake off the burden they bring to your brain.

Break up, out, through and free of this energetic drain. Create peace for yourself and everyone else around you. You already know there is no sense in saying the same things again to them, so stop trying.

Some people are addicted to chaos. Let them be and be not disturbed or perturbed any longer.

S.O.S.

Stuck on Stupid

How many licks does it take to get the thinking part of their brain?

You have to be willing to see what is going on and decide:

Do you want MORE of this or LESS of this?

Unless you LOVE a challenge...

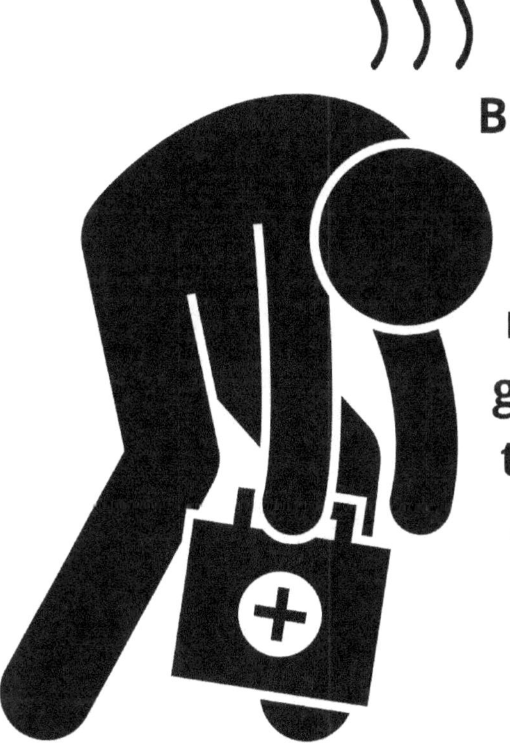

"Romeo the Suicidal Parakeet"

Based on real life 'bird dropping episodes' of Steve Kidd's bird.
Find it here: https://amzn.to/3FdoZs3

RED FLAG #5:

Erratic behavior

Erratic

Hit-or-miss; lacking consistency, regularity, or uniformity; irregular in performance, behavior, or attitude; inconsistent and unpredictable.

The obvious: you see someone driving erratically, or losing their mind at the grocery. You can avoid being harmed by keeping your distance. Whew.

My friend was cut-off on the highway. He honked and the 'offending' car fired back, literally. Bullets hit his car; bullets hit theirs. Apparently these dumbasses had just stolen that car and did what anybody would do: drive erratically and open fire on others. Sheesh.

"Erratic behavior" is one of the traits of a dumbass that really needs to be sussed-out as fast as possible.

When you get a good vibe from someone, you don't question it, right?

If you get a bad vibe from someone, don't second-guess it. Right on! Move on.

Go with your gut instinct. And then just GO.

Help a brother out if s/he needs it, of course. However, the global chaos that is our world is revealing some wack erratic shit right now. Don't be scared, be prepared.

PROACTIVE TIP: practice your responses before you need them.

Start using "OH, OK" out loud. It should make you smile if you do it right.

On a larger scale, take note of the leaders and businesses changing their tunes all erratic-like lately, amounting to being unpredictable in places where that just shouldn't be the case. They do not deserve a spot on anyone's team let alone the authority role they have assumed to have over you.

We are watching 'clown world' on parade. Laugh at them. Don't listen to them. They don't have a right to dictate what is right for you in any way, shape or form.

Erratic is dangerous. They play with your health, wealth and happiness.

Willy-nilly is not a leader. Liars are not leaders, either. If you only hear half the truth, what's the other half?

Erratic is Scary

Kristin is a 42 year old child and the poster child for erratic behavior. She is nice then she's mean, then full of apologies. Her judgment is horrible, having brought homeless people to her home. That's fine, except that later they were found roaming the property peeping into people's windows.

On this particular day, though, she really lost it:
"Did you hear what happened to me??" Oh God. NOW what?
"I saw a guy on the highway standing next to his car." She must have hit the brakes pretty hard to stop and pick him up. "His car broke down. I just wanted to help." So, she did what she does: she brought him home to wait for his friend to arrive.

"He just sat there on the couch like a statue. It was weird! Suddenly, he got up and left. I thought his friend came early, so I went to bed. In the morning, I realized my car was gone."

"I had a feeling I shouldn't bring him home but I didn't know what else to do." Well, it wasn't *that*...

The erratic behavior of
a dumbass can impact
even the innocent.
Avoid these people!!

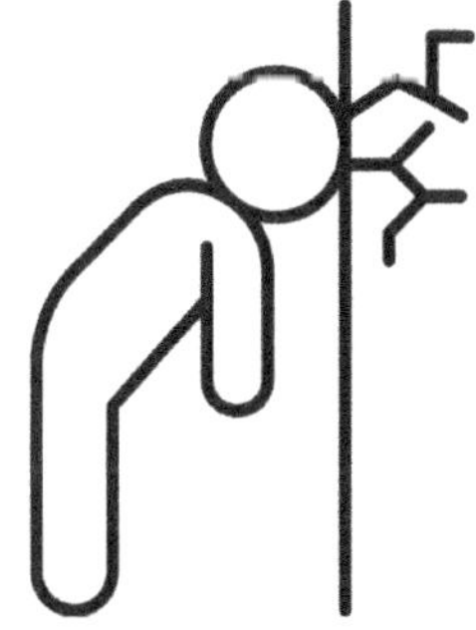

You are encouraged to look up the opposites of these five traits. It will open your eyes, giving you more options and criteria.

Isn't it interesting how intertwined these traits are?

❖   *Repeat Offenders* are that way because they are, in part, *Weak-Willed.*

❖   By definition, "not doing what you should," *Asleep at the Wheel,* is a form of *Apathy.*

❖   *Apathetic* types often display *Erratic* behavior. They just don't care what they do to you.

Even if it appears that "everyone is doing it" it does not have to apply to YOU. Think and act for yourself. Be your own stand-up guy. It takes guts to buck the B.S., but the alternative can be deadly. Not kidding even a little bit. Be careful who you trust, give allegiance to, and herald. They might not deserve it.

3 PROACTIVE STEPS

Seeing These Traits Ahead Of Time Is A Superpower. You Can Read The Writing On The Wall Before You Hit The Wall.

DO THE 3-STEP:

No doubt more shockers and shocking people will be headed our collective way. My vision is that we all respond with less 'knee-the-jerk' reaction and more calm.

No matter what, (but especially if you get riled-up!), look at it objectively. If a pencil fell off the table, what would that mean? Nothing. Unless you decide it means something, of course. If you have a dumbass in your life doing stupid people tricks, it means you have extra stupid stuff in your life that is optional. Like a toddler with a rattle, all that toddler can do is shake their rattle...they cannot do math or make wise choices. With compassion, you excuse yourself, or them, from the table.

"OHHH, OK" it's like that, eh? This response will help you keep your cool. No matter the matter, start here:

1. "OH, OK"
2. Do you want 'more' or 'less' of 'it'?
3. Move your feet accordingly.

When it comes to "move your feet accordingly," what will you do? What *can* you do?

You know you deserve to be treated with respect to your body, mind and spirit. Not everyone is capable, nor are they 'driven' to treat you as such. Take your time and notice the signs because the small things matter. Be quick to dismiss 'DUH' before it takes a dump in your life.

It's clear that what is happening to us all on a global scale really IS happening. It's hard not to feel angry, betrayed or powerless, like a sitting duck. There are things you can do. For one, stay away from anything metaverse or related. The movement to transform humans into machines started with payload delivery system they marketed as "for the greater good get your ___." Why would anyone buy into four different companies making a formula for the very same illness? It makes no sense. They are, therefore, sense-LESS. Call it like you see it, too, wherever and however it shows up. This is how you become a stand-up guy. Show 'em how it's done, hon.

Walk away. Do not consent to the concepts or pressures of others who clearly did not research or care enough to notice the ineffectiveness of simple things like a mask. It's been proven over and over again these do not work to block out or prevent transmission of anything but maybe spit. However, it does reduce oxygen levels and the nasty face diapers harbor all sorts of bacteria. OH OK then.

5 WAYS TO DEAL WITH A DUMBASS

What to do and say when they come your way.

Learn new ways to respond so you can stay "in the zone."

5 Ways to Deal with a Dumbass
be A.W.A.R.E.

AVOID: This might include not walking into that store, alleyway or relationship. Trust and follow your gut instinct.

WIT: Laughter is truly the best medicine. A witty response or just a laugh to yourself, it doesn't matter...both will benefit *you*.

ATTITUDE: Show that you mean business. Remember, a dumbass isn't that dialed-in so you might have to turn up the volume to be heard!

REPORT 'EM: If a dumbass continues to 'wreck the set' you have no choice but to report it. Please do. *It helps those who can help you* if/when things get out of control.

EXIT: Get out of their reach. You deserve better.

YOUR BEST MOVE

AVOID potholes and the people who dig them

Everyone deserves a chance or two, depending on how badly the first 'blowout' was, of course. Getting back into the ring with someone who is not interested is a waste of time for both of you. "Don't cast your pearls before swine" is profound and true. Look it up. It isn't being judgmental, it is using good judgment.

The people you love most can become an obstacle for you, an emotional sinkhole. It might be time to love from a distance so you don't fall into the potholes they create.

Separate yourself from human hammers because they see everything, and everyone, as a nail. It's tough love at times, but it sure beats getting beat-up.

The following are five ways you can deal with the people who would happily run your life if you let them.

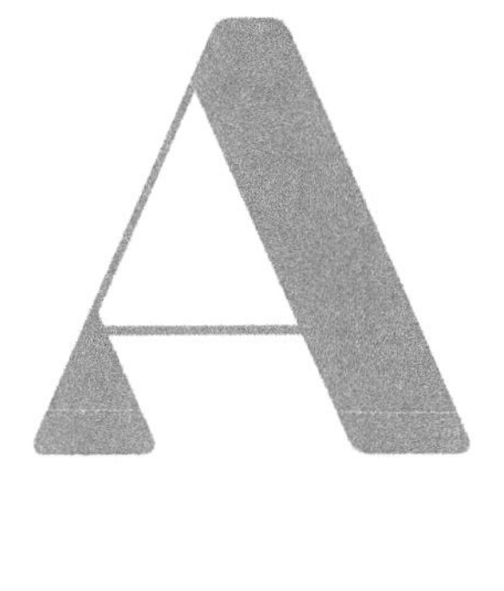

Avoid

You would park your new car away from other cars to avoid damage - do the same for yourself.

It's best to minimize engagement with a dumbass, or avoid altogether.

You won't be missing anything.

Knowledge is knowing a tomato is fruit.

Wisdom is not putting it in a fruit salad.

AVOID

MYTH: If I avoid someone they won't like me anymore.

THE PROBLEM: Does it matter? Chances are your dumbass doesn't even notice it. Remember they are often asleep at the wheel and apathetic people, anyway.

THE FIX: find yourself in the company of authentic and savvy people who "get you."

Over time, walls drop and true colors show. So, while your first impression is, "nice person," and you want to tell them all your family secrets, don't. People can change when they sense your guard is down. To them, your openness might be their cue to start 'swinging a cat by its tail' for all you know. It takes time to really know if someone is genuinely nice or if they are putting on a show. Sometimes, it takes no time at all. Check this out:

I had my doubts already. Tall, handsome, entertaining, flashy - all the right 'parts' to lure in a woman. I noticed he was rude to the bartender, but hey, he'd had a long day working the trade show. I understood. What I mean is, I cut him a bunch of slack.

Not wanting to be rude (people pleaser alert), I stayed to have tapas with him. Have you ever found yourself apologizing to the waiter for your date's obnoxiousness? It was like that. The initial 'spark' I felt when we met at the trade show was now a nervous little flame. It didn't help that he kept whispering about sex-acts he had in mind. What a guy.

But old habits die hard, so I cut him some more slack. I'd been hoping to meet Mr. Right which 'made' me more open to accepting flaws. Why? I dunno. I guess that's what we do when we lower our standards: we accept the unthinkable. We override that 'uh oh' feeling, opting for rose-colored glasses and hope it works out. That's like hoping you can get orange juice from a cow, and that it comes out cold, too.

That night I was still excited by the possibility that maybe, just maybe, I'd met a great guy in spite of the red flags on the field. I just wasn't sure. It was too soon to tell - or was it?

When in doubt wait it out.

If it isn't a BIG Yes, there are elements of a no.
Trust this much is true:

It'll be greater later.

Sign me up

I want to encourage you to do what I did: ask for a sign. Sincerely invite divine intervention into your situation and be willing to make a move based on that sign. Be open to being completely wrong about your first impression. Honor yourself by respecting that higher know-how's guidance to, or away from, a situation.

I went to bed, excited - or was that fear? Lol. It can be hard to discern the difference, at times. Here's what to gather from those moments: if it isn't a "BIG YES!" then it's a "NO." Am I aware that I've repeated myself here? Heck yes I am - it's for a reason: living by *your* "BIG Yes!" is going to help you to avoid some royal jackasses in life.

Here is what happened with that man I met at the tradeshow after I prayed for a sign. It wasn't the answer I was hoping for, that's for sure...

Sidestepping a Pothole:

He: "Would you like to have dinner with me?"

Me: Sure! How about if we pick back up with the original plans to meet at Chesapeake;s Seafood? What time shall we meet?

He: "I don't feel like seafood today."

Oh, OK. Where might you have in mind? I'll meet you there, instead.

"I feel like steak but you don't like that much, do ya?"

It's fine! I know I can find something to eat.

"This isn't going to work out."

Well, maybe I can think of a spot to meet?

"No. You won't let me come pick you up! Why the hell won't you let me pick you up??! What is it: Are you ashamed of where you live or something? I just don't get it!!"

click

Then he called back to yell at me about how messed up dating was and how paranoid I must be.

Whoa. It's a good thing this happened! I'd already agreed to a long mountain drive with him for the following day. You see: I was going on first impressions but it's the last one that matters more.

Can you imagine being stuck at the top of a mountain with a man like this as your driver?

CASE STUDY: TANYA'S DILEMMA

Tanya called me crying. She was FED UP with five women who called to vent, rant or ask for favors. This went on for years. "When I need something, they aren't available. When holidays come around, they don't even respond to my text messages. They don't ask about my kids; they call to say they are dropping-off theirs for the day. I'm sick of it!! But what can I do? They call when I tell them not to, and leave nasty messages if I don't get back to them fast enough. This is stressing me out! I feel helpless to change any of it. HELP ME."

A genuinely sweet person, Tanya is a single mother of three boys; has taken on raising two nephews; is doing her best to make it. She was always there for the apathetic crew. In spite of her requests in the past, these women had no intentions of respecting her boundaries.

Taking the bull by the horns with them was not something she wanted to do: she *had* to do it.

We decided to create some automated messages so the next time one of them called she could put them off in a new way. It was hard, at first, to consider that she might be seen as rude. Reflecting on how apathetic all of them were toward her, and how, if she didn't do something different it would continue, she agreed to a change.

We had fun revising automated text messages to: "I already told you I am busy right now." They would always call back, so we got ready; the second message was simple: "I'm still busy. I'll call you later, maybe." Third: "I said I would call you back when I have time." And finally: "I don't have time for this anymore."

Here's what happened: nothing. All of a sudden, the calls stopped. She never had to send one of those 'rude' messages but she was ready. Awareness + Acceptance + Action = Change.

It was like her determination to avoid more of their crap went out and 'touched someone' - all five someone's, in fact. Pretty cool, huh?

Forgive yourself for leaving the barnyard gate open or ignoring those hunches you had all along. Live and learn. Let them go. Wracking your brain over the past won't solve much.

As the saying goes, "Rejection is God's protection," so you're doing them a favor. Ok, soo, maybe that's a reach. You get my point. You don't have to apologize for making better choices. In fact, you need to 'reject to protect' your own self, too.

What IS is what shows up.
What you make of it is up to you.

All you really need to
do is 'handle' it,
not understand it.

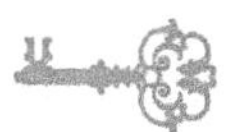

Delete the need to understand.

Compassion is a great trait but sticking around to 'grasp' the reasons for a dumbass doing dumbass things does *not change a dumbass thing.*

He knows it all, just ask him.
I called my father from Australia to ask his advice about moving forward with Tim. He and I had been having some issues and here I was at 47 years old, hoping I'd finally found the right man...*but.* Bragging about his 24 year marriage the entire 24 years, I figured Pops would be my 'Dr. Phil.' She was his fourth wife; it appeared he earned the 'position' of authority.

ME: Dad, am I making the right decision or were these red flags?

He: "What's Tim's last name?"

"Cox. Why Dad?

"That doesn't sound Aboriginal. Just marry him."

Wait, wut? 'Mr. MENSA,' the smartest man in any room - just ask him - just said *that* after I poured my heart out to him? I was desperate for answers, insights, wisdom - anything but a racist remark. I listened to Dad, overrode my concerns, and married Tim. It was not a "BIG Yes!" but I loved him so much I thought marriage would calm things down.

I should have listened to my gut, not my father. That marriage went to hell in a handbasket on our honeymoon. Yes, that night he showed his true colors and it only got worse, not better, as I had hoped.

Turns out Tim was an abusive man who showed me the ropes on domestic violence. I bet his previous wives could have told me that. Can you imagine living in a foreign country and discovering you've married an abuser? It could have been avoided but I gave away my power to Dad, the *not*-know-it-all.

Later in life it was discovered that dear old dad didn't have a marriage made in heaven. He confessed to me, from his deathbed, that his wife was a liar on just about every level. So, all this time, bragging about how great his marriage was - how flawless everything seemed to be - was all a lie, too, huh? I couldn't find those words, nor would I say that to a dying man... but damn.

The person I trusted for guidance was full of shit. I overrode everything I felt in favor of a person who turned out to be an arrogant liar. Owning my role in this means I failed the test; would have/should have Monday night quarterback... whatever...it felt 'off.'

PROACTIVE TIP: When you are taxed emotionally you can't think that clearly.

Witty comebacks do not come to mind, either. Pick a few one-liners and commit them to heart.

The next section, as well as "Attitude," will help get you ready for the next time.

REAL LIFE: WHAT TO SAY WHEN THEY COME YOUR WAY

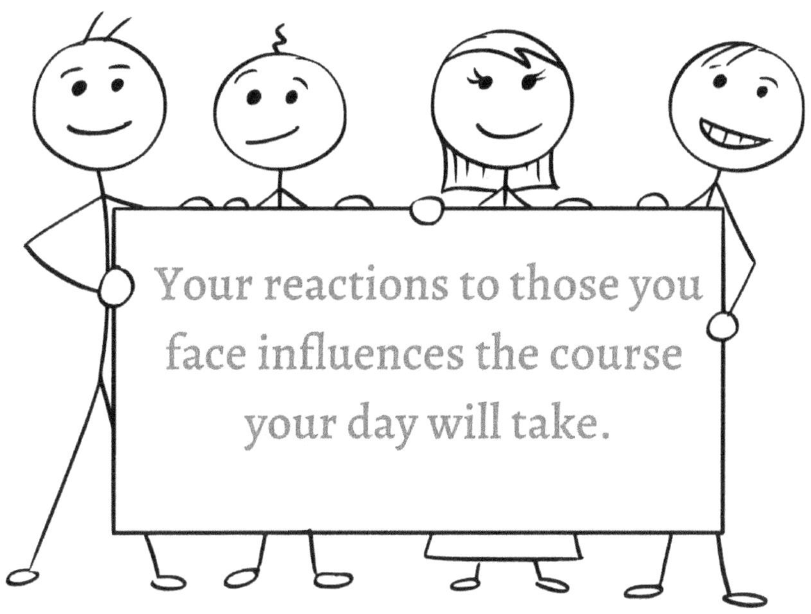

What you want is to be as neutral as possible. That's why this is so powerful: because it helps you accept what shows up without judging it.

You simply say "OHHH, OK."

The simplest way to respond:

"OH, OK!"

Regardless of what you witness,
accepting it on an "as is" basis
helps YOU stay calm.
Instead of getting mad or
whatever, just say, "OH, OK, then"
to yourself.
Try to find the laugh in it ASAP.

"Do I want *more* of this or *less* of this?"

move your feet accordingly

How many times have you said, "I *knew it. I knew* I should/ shouldn't have done that!" -? It's *you* who pays for it, so listen to yourself more than the cymbal-clanging monkeys on the playground. They don't know what's right for you to do, do they?

Who pays for it later? Regret is one helluva weight to carry around and it isn't just you who pays the price. The tax and toll on your mind impacts everyone in your circle. It demonstrates to others (and your kids) how to treat you and how it's OK to let others treat them.

Nearly 100% of the time regret comes from overriding your "still, small voice." Can you think of a time when you regretted listening to your intuition? Nah, didn't think so.

And yet, we all do it. So forgive yourself for being pressured or gullible or whatever it was that made you ignore your hunches. Beating yourself up with "I should have known better" doesn't heal a wound, it keeps it open. It lowers your vibe, self-confidence and clarity, too.

Just decide, for once, that it is OK to be viewed as rude or what the F-ever in other people's eyes. So what. They're not the boss of you.

BEER PRESSURE

I was living in Australia and only knew a few people at first: fun folks I met at the pub, of course. This particular night one of them asked me to drive her 2 blocks to the drive-in liquor store. We just had a tequila shot. One. I let them 'push' me to drive even though I said 'no' at first. TWO blocks. I could have walked but they wouldn't serve a walk-up. So, I drove and, when pulling away from the shop, got the dreaded 'blue light special.' The cop was a real jerk, but hey, I was 1/10th % over the new legal limit.

"You got the worst cop on the force" I heard later. I was belligerent AF. In the end, he went home from work, and I spent the night on a cold slab of cement. Not a great view with the bars all around, you know? This one mistake cost thousands in legal fees and nearly the approval of my work visa.

Here's the thing I want to own up to: life in AUS was stressful from Day 1. The work visa depended on a boss, an American no less (they call us "Bloody yank, septic tank"); he was someone *nobody* liked, and he put the squeeze on me daily. "You came in here all bright and happy honey but now you look like a kicked dog." That was just one patient's comment. A nightmare marriage, crappy job situation, feeling trapped, stuck, beat-up by life - it is any wonder I attracted the worst cop on the force? When we are upset our vibration bottoms-out and we attract the bottom of the barrel.

Inevitably, when things go awry it started with ignoring the nudges and "NO's." So much could have been avoided. With all that negativity around me, I'm surprised people weren't avoiding me. It gets old after a while even if the reason or cause is legit.

Please don't let a dumbass talk you into doing something you feel a 'no' about doing. You do not have to explain yourself to them. You've seen how far that got me, right? My weak-willed people-pleaser habits kicked-in and I got kicked in the ass for it.

Do you think these folks helped me get out of jail that night? Do you think they came to court or supported me through a *year* of legal hassles? The fact that they pushed for me to drive was the first red flag. I was the dumbass who did it. Their apathy is, and was, a foregone conclusion.

As you clear the field of monkeys you create space for new types of people to come along. There are people who would be like, "Oh, OK. If you're not feelin' it, that's fine! I'll figure out something else." It's clean. It's simple. It's easy. And it works in your favor. Find a way to say no!

NICE WAYS TO SAY "NO THANKS!"

Real life brings us all sorts of opportunities to speak with integrity. But man, it can be hard to do when fibbing comes so easily. That has its own issues, as you will see:

Hey, Frank! Wanna go to that party on Friday?

You are Frank. You don't want to go. You:
1. Say "Sure!" while planning to pull a no-show already. You realize you're going to have to stay out of sight that night.
2. Say, "I'm busy" then formulate a lie you'll have to cover for later just to get out of it.
3. Say, "Sure!" but everything about you is saying 'heck no.' You feel used already. Again.

You feel "used" because inside, your tiny little self inside, is screaming "NOOOOOO, not *again!!*" Plus, there is a ton of energy being spent here contriving a way out before the party's even started.

All you know is that you aren't 'feeling it' for the party. That's enough of a reason. Maybe you're 'supposed to be' somewhere else that night and your gut knows that already -?

Whatever the reason, instead of lying, back-peddling or being shady, try this:

"Thanks, man, but I'm just not feelin' it. You know how you gotta trust those things, right?" You smile. Change the topic. You don't have to explain yourself. All you have to know is this: when you are asked to do something, do you feel *a BIG Yes,* or not?

Hey, Frank! Would you like to pick me up at the airport again? You don't want to. In fact, you may be feeling taken advantage of - it's the fifteenth time or something and you are over it. What would you do?

1. Obligingly say 'ok' and feel resentment towards him for asking and towards yourself for saying 'ok' when it wasn't.
2. Say 'ok' to his face and cancel via text message when you get home, or worse, on the travel day itself.
3. Make up a lie on the spot. You'll have to remember what lie you told and maybe even include other people as your alibi or 'cover.' It gets messy.

Gratitude Sandwiches

Start out with something sincere (if you can muster it!): "Aww, thanks, man, I appreciate that you asked me to pick you up again but, _______."

OR: "You know I would love to, dude but, _______."

Smile when being a smartass. Deflect with humor. Give this a shot: "I would dude, but my rates have gone up and you can't afford me." Whatever your best 'but' is what works; at least you aren't saying 'yes' when it is a 'no.' Respect those hunches!

Once you start honoring yourself in these little moments by not doing something you don't want to do, you might be amazed at how the world starts to mirror back the same thing: respect. Since "like attracts like" your personal magnetism will begin drawing different people to you. Keep that 'bar' raised no matter who tries to lower it. Dumbasses can be pretty manipulative without even trying. There you are, just being a nice person and BAM! they gotcha. Be strong & *stick to your guns*.

The bonus is that you won't be busy doing stuff you never wanted to do in the first place. That minimizes resentment, remorse and regret. Would *you* want a friend showing up out of obligation, all sour-pussed and bad vibes? Of course not. Don't be *that guy*.

Now, I know all this stuff is like, 'duh!' but think about how you actually respond when faced with this dilemma. It can be hard to "keep it real." Prepare your best answer so you won't be taken by surprise next time.

If someone pries into your world you can always respond with, "Oh, well, that's a touchy topic I'd rather not discuss right now if you don't mind."

If you've got that 'nothing to lose' feeling, there are some real smartass remarks in the chapter on ATTITUDE.

"I'm not the marrying kind and I'm not going to bear your children…still want to buy me that drink?" lol

Of course, you could say, "I'm not getting a real BIG yes on that but if things change I'll let you know." Find your way to make a clean break. It is so much better than feeling obligated and later, resentful or worse, full of regret.

You know by now that the guilt and self-flagellation you'll be doing, adding salt to a wound that could have been avoided, is not worth the 'save face' fib in the moment.

STRATEGY #2

WiT for the Nitwits

Wit

Intelligent playfulness or humor in expression, as in speech, writing, or art.

Choose to be amused.

Tibor has been teaching children about
love in the face of hate. Ah-mazing!

You can find our interview on YouTube.
He's sassy-sweet & inspiring!

"...when you put your life in a good place, good things follow."

— Willie Nelson

Handling a dumbass with witty comebacks is not the only way to use this idea. What I have found is that it is better to find one's own sense of humor first. In fact, this is the single best question you could ask of your day, multiple times a day, even.

THE BEST QUESTION YOU COULD EVER ASK:

"How can I have more fun today than I ever thought possible?"

This question produces results without any effort on your part.
Just ask, then forget about it. Your day will improve, promise!

What you're doing here is resetting your vibration to a higher 'octave' if you will.

Stay focused on the 'what' and the 'how?' will make itself known.

Don't worry about 'making' the day fun; just let it come to you. It will, effortlessly.

This is under 'wit' because it'll get you to a better state of being.

Let's face it: dealing with a dumbass is not always a good time. By setting your mood you'll have better results.

This is true for each day, by the way. So many spiritual teachers tell you to 'see it, say it, let it go' and then forget about it. Go out and play. This is where most folks stumble: they're focused on the HOW of the WHAT they want. Stress sets in and it wrecks the set.

Imagine sitting at a restaurant, menu in hand. You pick Chicken Cacciatore. You don't see the kitchen but you know they are 'reassembling' themselves just to make your order. Not once does the waiter rush back to ask if you know how Chicken Cacciatore is made. You probably have no idea, right? It doesn't matter: it's on the menu. The 'Universal Kitchen' will take care of making it for you.

Making stuff manifest begins with a good mood and a good idea of what you want. Mostly what we want is to feel good. That's why this question is truly the best one you could ask, then follow through on when the hunches start rolling in. LET it lead you.

This works or your money back.
JK

"What's funny about this that I haven't noticed, yet?"

Tony Robbins was able to pull himself out of depression after his partner embezzled everything, he got fat and was being evicted. How? This one question got him laughing again.

P.S. Lost keys? Ask repeatedly: "Where haven't I looked, yet?"

MYTH: You have to take all of this stupidity very seriously.

THE TRUTH: These people are stuck on stupid but you don't have to be.

THE FIX: find your funny bone again. Seriously. The sooner you can find a way back to center, back to being light-hearted, the better you can deal with a total dumbass.

Smile, then dial

It was 10:20PM on a Friday night when I heard a soft knock at the door. And then, "Lonneeeeeee" being called over and over again. It was Kristin. Oh God, now what? Soon, the knocks turned into her scratching the door. Long scratches from top-to-bottom - enough to drive ya crazy. "Lonneeeeee." This went on for a full 20 minutes as I sat paralyzed, unable to concentrate. If I opened that door I probably would have regretted my knee-that-jerk response. Was it warranted? Heck yeah. I was furious with her for being so disrespectful. She'd already been told "NO, we are not friends; NO, we will never hang out; NO, I will not come over and NO, you will never be invited into my home again."

Fortunately, another neighbor entered the building. I could hear their conversation - in fact, it was 11PM when things got quiet outside my door. Kristin had been yelling to her from my door the whole time. I sat in fear that the knocking would start up again. It did not. Oh thank God.

The next day I decided to say something. Advance planning really helped me stick to the 'script.' Part of that was resetting my mood and attitude. I wanted to box her ears, I swear. Instead, I did a couple of these things from the playlist that follows. And I had to remind myself, "love away your enemies" over and over again.

I put on some lipstick and music that makes me happy. I've learned it doesn't work to show up with a scowl.

When I knocked at her door she tried to put me off. "I'm busy! I don't have time right now."

(as if I had time the night before) Errgh! "I don't care, Kristin." I forced a smile. "We are going to agree, *right now*, that what you did last night will never happen again, *aren't we?* We AGREE that you will never *ever* come to my door again, *right?*" She looked dumbfounded and denied it. Apparently alcohol causes memory loss. I took a deep breath and reminded her of the long-winded conversation she had with our neighbor outside my door. The lights went on. "Ohhhh, yeahhhh."

"You clawed, scratched and called-out my name for 20 minutes last night, Kristin." I was doing my best to keep cool and continued to speak to her simply, softly and kind. "So we agree, right now, that you will never, *ever* do that again, *don't we?*"

A barrage of apologies followed as I turned and walked away from her door. "The best apology is changed behavior, Kristin!" was all I could muster without getting madder. It was hard to do, I'm not going to lie, but the sense of accomplishment was worth every bit of effort.

Confronting a dumbass comes with a whole bunch of stress, I know, but if you don't do it, you pay for it later. The best way to deal with them is from a peaceful place.

Sure, you wanna throttle stupid; attack in self-defense. No, it doesn't make sense *why* someone treats you like they do. Delete the need to understand. I know they can bring you down. That is why I created this list - a way to reset, recenter, recalibrate - whatever 're' you need to do to get back to feeling good, *first*.

Truly, this is the space where your best decisions are made anyway. This is the vibe you want to have as much as possible: UPBEAT.

They say we are here to become great manifestors, among other things. By following your "BIG Yes!" and hunches, you can do more activation of your innate power to create or alter your world.

You can do it. You've been doing it! Just look around you and notice the ways you've changed, be it yourself or the stuff in your world.

Name it.

Claim it.

Make it so.

All so much easier to do

When you're in the flow.

Here are some ideas that'll help restore your sanity when things get a little crazy out there for ya:

THE 'CHEAPER THAN THERAPY' PLAYLIST

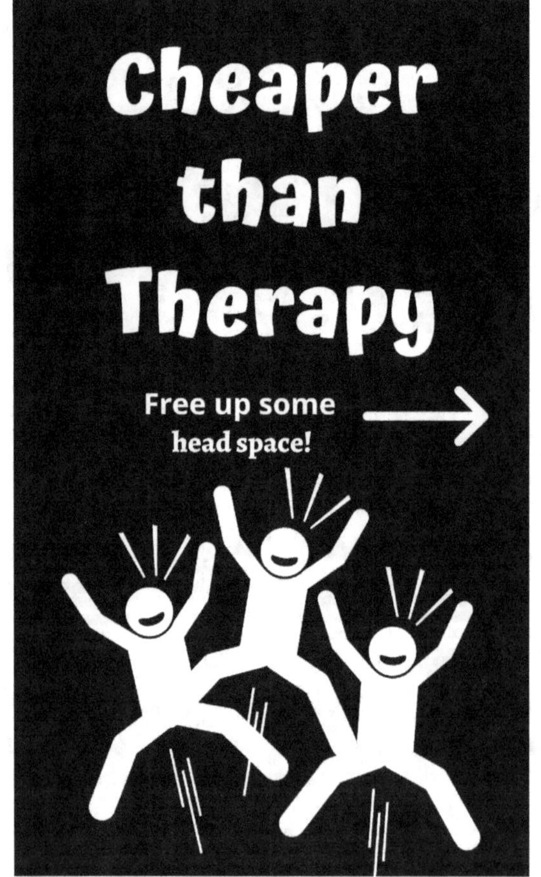

Here's the Playlist - a way to find yourself - or lose yourself as the case may be - in groovy music or lash-out by smashing cheap burner plates on the counter. Whatever it takes to find your happy place again is worth doing *before* you take that bull by the horns. I mean it: find a way to get happy again. Your vibration is the center of everything, so stay centered. Here are some ideas you can implement for free:

Since everybody recommends meditation, you won't find it mentioned. It works, but when you feel upset, sitting down to cite 'aum' might not be an option. These are ways you can re-center and *then* deal with a dumbass:

1. *Ask,* ***"How can I have more fun today than I ever thought possible?"*** Your brain works to answer the questions you ask of it, so use *this* one to reset the rest of your day. It's effortless and it works. The reason you want to get back to "fun" is so your creativity can flow, your vibe stays high, and your ability to handle a dumbass is enhanced. Ask this question any time, or any number of times in the day when you feel derailed.

2. *Tunes!* Play music that moves you. I go for "Na na na, hey, hey, hey," "For What It's Worth" by Buffalo Springfield, and "Kickin' up Mud" by the hick-hop group, The LACS (which stands for Lazy Ass Crackers.) You gotta see that video: it's a redneck party in the field fo'sho'. You might love swing music. Whatever it is, make sure you choose upbeat, not sad, OK? Then put your fav on repeat. Who cares?? Use it to elevate you ASAP. Let it take you to a happy place. **TO DO: start building that go-to music playlist this week. Put it on a USB stick as back-up, too, by the way.** You can't always count on the internet…and that's exactly the time you'll be wanting a 'groovy tune' to keep you upbeat! Music uplifts so play it!

3. *Rebuild your faith in YOU*. Confirm your ability to manifest! Look around you and notice all that you have manifested. *You are powerful no matter how you feel right now.* Delight

in your own power to transform; know that you can handle this. Look for evidence in your life already - of how you've managed to manifest outcomes in your favor before; know that you can do it again. Write down the cool stuff you've done or the accomplishments you've achieved. Boost your own ego. Besides, 'confidence' is sexy.

4. ***Tapping.*** Become your own healer by learning the 5 minute tapping routine. A near fix-all for most issues, (anxiety, pain, phobias, sadness), it will help whether or not you believe it will. This technique is easy to learn and you can do it anywhere. I do this while I'm driving - it might stress out other people around me (lol!) but so what? I feel better in the moment and the next day, too! My video routine: https://youtu.be/Q8yVih75Wc4.

5. ***Gift yourself with a present.*** THE present. "NOW" is all we have. If you catch yourself reviewing or even futuring an interaction with a dumbass, get back to the 'here and now.' I find that consciously breathing in the word 'light' and exhaling 'love' really helps. Pick words that work for you. Be really *really* present. Some folks write or say 10 gratitudes out loud. This puts you in the moment, too. Revisit #1 to reset your day's vibe.

6. ***Sound off.*** Let's face it, the sound of leaf blowers outside might be enough to put you over the edge. Or someone's voice - a song or a beat - these can get under your skin worse than a freakin' tick. It's time to change the channel. Sitting in the car, where sound is minimized, *with the stereo on*, works pretty well for a temporary escape. The bottom line: *adjust.* For sensitive types like us, sounds can truly make you squirm. If it is someone's incessant talking then you've got to figure out how to shut 'em up without a squabble. It might mean you relocate but it'd be worth your sanity. Ask yourself, "Do I want more of this or less of this?" "This" might be the feeling or the source of irritation. What

matters most is *you* getting centered once again.

7. ***Cafe Amor.*** Show yourself some love with a steaming cuppa. Will it be tea, or tequila, darlin'? Who cares? I knew a man who boasted about quitting drinking when his children were little. That was 40 years ago. "I really *love* Scotch." Then have some Scotch, brother. If you were on your deathbed tomorrow would you be glad you denied yourself all these years, long after the kids have grown and left home? Doubt it.

8. ***Put on some lipstick.*** Ladies, this works. If you work from home, like I do, it's too easy to look (and feel) like a slouch. When I feel like crap, I reach for the paisley bell bottoms, fluff up my new shag haircut to look 70s cool, cover the dark circles and put on some eyeliner. This is a form of self-love when you make yourself look a bit fancy, I think. Just do it for you and watch your mood improve. Fill up your own cup and you have more to give. It isn't selfish, *it's essential.*

9. ***Vent.*** Have a venting buddy!! The understanding is that you just vent, they just listen. No advice is given. Let 'er rip, baby! Here's another idea: physically slamming a cheap metal burner plate cover on the counter is actually quite rewarding for most all the senses. I mean it. Don't knock it til ya try it. The sound of smashing plates on a brick wall would be ideal, of course. That was my fantasy: a place you could go to rage out. I called it the A.R.C. - the Anger Release Center. I hear there are places like this nowadays: "rage bars." For one dollar, you can get three loud burner plates - have your way with those instead of someone you'd love to trash. **Cheap thrills, baby.** Get 'em when you can. It is your job to let that stuff go and get back to feeling UP ASAP.

10. ***Take a walk on the wild side.*** Nature rocks. Put your spine up against a tree trunk and ask the tree to remove your pain, stress, etc. Run those toes through some grass or plop down

on the moss and take a break. Send your stress into the earth and watch it go to work. This even helps with physical pains, by the way. Watch the movie, *"Earthing."*

11. ***Sparks of truth.*** Wit behind truth: *Awaken with JP* tackles our global topics and idiots with genius-level creativity and humor. Also, this is a personal playlist filled with inspiring, enlightening, 'reminders' I think you'll enjoy. It is on my YouTube channel: https://bit.ly/deepthinkersset.

12. ***Invite Divine Intervention.*** THIS saved my life. It's a story worth sharing and you can find it on the new podcast, "How to Deal with a Dumbass." Whatever version of 'Let Go, Let God' you prefer works, but *you have to invite - give consent -* and then watch what happens for you. Ask for a clear sign if you are not sure about a person, place or thing you might do. Invite Divine Intervention into your world and expect to be amazed.

13. ***LOL.*** Jumping baby goat videos, screaming sheep and fainting pygmies are *hysterical* videos. *Dry Bar Comedy Channel* "How to Cope in a World Full of Idiots" on YouTube has good, clean humor so you don't have to worry if the kids can hear it. *Laugh Planet* has good clips to get you laughing, as well. Reuniting with owners, this compilation will have you tearful and laughing all at once. You have got to hear Einstein the bird talk/sound human! Check out *The Dodo* or *Cutest Animals #37,* too. For Netflix lovers: keyword "witty" or "irreverent" and then pick "witty comedies" or "irreverent award winning movies" to get a 'leg up' on your cinematic time-out.

14. ***Breathe.*** When rough seas hit we hit the deck and become shallow breathers. This restricts your soul, they say. IDK who "they" is but I do know this much: deep inhales, imagining light or love coming in with deep exhales, imagining all the stress leaving you, *really works.* Combine it with putting your bare feet on the earth. It's a great

combo. Wim Hof, "The Ice Man," has breathing techniques you can easily do, right now, for free, that are game-changers. In fact, he has helped thousands of people with verifiable psychosis to completely heal themselves and toss out those medications. Wow!

15. **_Ribbon Cutting Ceremony._** Ties that bind for a long time need to be cut, releasing that person and clearing up your energy field once again. Here is what you do: imagine yourself and the external person/source that is a royal pain in butt. Go ahead and call it what it is, OK? Give yourself permission to cut those cords between you. SEE the cord connecting you to that person. Then imagine a gigantic pair of scissors in your hands. You know, the kind they use at grand opening ceremonies to cut that ribbon? Yes, like that: oversized to the max. SEE your hands on the handles and cut that cord between you and them. WATCH them float away, getting smaller and smaller. Wave bubye to that shrinking image. Continue doing ribbon cuttings for any source of irritation or angst, be it past or present. Honestly, this works so well _and_ you don't even have to understand it. Just do it. See #1, next.

16. **_Write your heart out._** Writing gets 'it' out of your head and onto paper where you can better deal with 'it.' Write letters you will never send. Let your emotions rage, roar and reveal how you truly feel. You gotta let it out to get it out. Have your say and be on your way. My book, "Life lessons learned from a lousy mother," was inspired by the time I tried to write a Mother's Day card of gratitude for all the wonderful things my mother taught me. I couldn't think of anything. It was blank. While that was a sad truth, it was acknowledging how I really felt…and _then_ healing can fill the place of the release. Once you 'have' something you can let it go.

17. **_Listen to a podcast._** Push away from your desk,

(or that person) and tune into something else for a bit. If you'd like to hear a laugh that makes you laugh, check out: **Do NOT feed the animals https://anchor.fm/howtodealwithadumbass/episodes/Dont-Feed-the-Animals-e1dblpf**

18. *Follow your "BIG Yes!"* It might defy logic or seem crazy to other people, but it works out in your favor. Your BIG Yes! might not be evident at this moment - the one where you've gotten blown off course or blown-away by somebody's 'stuff.' That's OK. When in doubt, wait it out. Delete the need to understand. Let nature take its course. Ask for signs. Even if you don't know what is next, remember, that is still knowing something: what you don't want to have ever again! It is part of the honing process in life, deciding what is best, next. See #1.

SUGGESTED WIT FOR DEALING WITH NITWITS

People can astonish you with epic stupidity. It proves there must be a God looking out for everyone because they 'made it' somehow, bless their little hearts.

We've already discussed how keeping up your own vibe is the point of this book. That said, I just wanted to offer-up some snarky comebacks you might love to use but won't, right? Definitely maybe.

1. *How* did you get this far?
2. You're not stupid! You just have bad luck when you're thinking.
3. Were you born this stupid or did you take lessons?
4. If ignorance is bliss, you must be the happiest person on the planet.
5. You're the reason God created the middle finger.
6. Stupidity isn't a crime so you're free to go.
7. Aww, it's so cute when you try to talk about things you don't understand.
8. I was hoping for a battle of wits but you appear to be unarmed.
9. People like you are the reason I'm on medication.
10. Remember when I asked for your opinion? Me neither.

11. You're impossible to underestimate.
12. I don't have the time or the crayons to explain this to you.

Stan Fields: "Describe your perfect date."

Cheryl: "That's a tough one. I'd have to say April 25. Because it's not too hot and not too cold. All you need is a light jacket."

—Stan Fields (William Shatner) and Cheryl Frasier (Heather Burns), *Miss Congeniality*

STRATEGY #3 FOR DEALING WITH DIM-ASSES

ATTITUDE

Detangle with a new angle

Attitude

Stop being sooo nice to those who don't return it but will keep asking you to give them more.

ATTITUDE

MYTH: If you are really super nice then people will treat you the same way in return.

THE TRUTH: Not everyone on planet earth is going to be a "good person" and appreciate you trying to be kind to them.

THE FIX: You may have to raise your voice to get rid of the deaf, dumb and willfully-blind.

A new attitude toward an old problem is always a good idea...

White Lies to Survive?

Ladies, you know this better than anyone: tell a dude 'no' and watch his true colors show. Guys, if you were smart about this you would realize that it may not be a 'forever no,' just a 'not right now no.' Gals, you gotta be clear. If you are, and the men still aren't listening, it is time to cop an attitude. Go bolder than you have before to get new results.

For the meek and mild-mannered, "attitude" might be getting up to use the loo at the bar but never coming back. It might mean ghosting someone. (see 'Avoid' for what to do when they pursue you anyway.) I'm not advocating for this technique. Just offering options is all.

If you're fed up, have nothing to lose, and truly are 'over it,' you may also be unnecessarily rough on the toddler. Careful there: being brutal feels good but it can have repercussions you don't want. You're gonna have to gauge it for yourself just how "done" you are. The best advice is to respond from neutral gear, of course.

For the bold, it might mean smartass comebacks like, "You want me to do what?? I've been *paid* for less, mate." Turn on your spike heel and bounce, gurl.

Maybe you don't care to be 'hit on' and clearly the dumbass doesn't take hints very well. You could lean in to whisper (or shout), "I can't. You look like my ___," (closest relative) and that would be weird. I'm sure you understand."

No one likes to be rejected or ghosted, so expect some flack or pushback when you act out of the norm. Expect the self-proclaimed authority to manipulate, sulk, or hurl blame back at you. One of the fastest ways to know a person is by their reaction to you setting a boundary; saying 'not this time.'

Being "professional" at work makes 'attitude' tricky: you have to decide the value of the relationship. Do you want to keep it intact? Then be tactful. Apply liberal use of "OH, OK" and long walks. Air boxing does wonders for the mind, body and soul. Just don't do it at the office.

ON THE HOMEFRONT

As children, it is natural to put our parents on a pedestal. They are our first authority figures but that does not automatically make them your best resource for life. For years, I tried to reconcile with a mother who made it clear from an early age that she had it out for her daughter. Even as late as my 50s, my mother would mimic, mock and joke at my expense. During the one and only time I stood up for myself and yelled back, (after *decades* of taking it on the chin), it did absolutely nothing. It fell on deaf ears. The next day she confessed to holding onto grudges from when I was nine years old. That was a 40 year old resentment, man. **Life moves forward but not all people do.** Her attitude was far from warm-and-fuzzy. Why stand around and get clawed by the swinging cat again?

Move according to your newer, higher standards, please. Otherwise, it's like standing still and agreeing to be target practice, *again.*

Cut-and-run, hon.
As hard as it is to 'cop an attitude' about people we love, I am *urging* you to do just that if you must. Relationships need the balance of a win-win. Compassion for where someone 'is' does not obligate you to stay there with them.

As a 'professional tumbleweed' who moved on a whim (so?!) I was often accused of running away. Don't let people stop you from traveling or moving on, period. *What if you are actually 'moving toward,' instead?* Cutting bait is cutting losses, no matter how you frame it. Ain't no shame in that game.

"Attitude" for you might be cutting someone out of your life. GOOD. DO IT. Do yourself and the world-at-large a favor: get back to feeling good. That's where the magic lies. *This* is when you are freed up from the inside-out. It is, in my opinion, the path to true personal freedom. Take it or leave it.

They won't like it when you stop tolerating their stupid games. Oh well. You don't wanna put up with their stuff either, do you?

Cut-and-run, Hon...cut and run!

(sorry not sorry)

if being a "B" is what it takes to get results

then, be a "B"

(Don't) put a lid on it

I want to blow the lid off the concept that you should never be mad, no pun intended. If an elephant steps on your foot, even if he didn't mean to, you're going to hurt and probably get pissed. Sure you'll calm down, have compassion for the elephant, and life goes on. But let's hold up a second here: **have your feelings first.**

I used to get mad that I got mad. Boy, oh, boy, if you wanna paint yourself into a corner just try that 'trick.' It is soo not fair to do that to yourself. Chances are it is a learned behavior; the remains left by critical parents who never cut you a break. Put down the self-flagellation tools!

Look at it this way: if you got cut, you would bleed. You are a human being with feelings. Allow yourself to have them. Whatever they are, have them. You have to let it out to get it out, baby. It beats adopting "angry person" as your identity, that's for sure.

Take a look at the *Cheaper Than Therapy Playlist* idea #9: ***VENT!*** Physically expelling that energy is going to help you move through this stuff faster than if you stuff it inside where it will

Pester. Fester. BOOM!

Item #9 also suggests having a vent buddy that will listen to you. Once you feel heard you can entertain the absurd, the silly, and the stuff you *wish* you could have said to a dumbass.

My friend, Steve, is THE Snark Master, I swear. For instance, when I asked him, "What are some snarky ways to say 'NO' to a dumbass? You know, the one who keeps pushing as if you never said 'stop!'?" - this is what he sent me:

Aww, thanks for asking, but I would rather*:

Be shark bait
Start eating roadkill
Listen to only Gregorian chant
Stick pins in both eyes
Willingly be toothless
Go to prison and be someone's bitch
Kill myself, resurrect and do it again
Eat mildly maggoty bread
Walk on nails

Gargle with toilet water

***Stuff you'll probably never say to anyone, but hey, if it makes *you* laugh in *your head*, who cares?**

"I'd rather stick pins in both eyes." Or, "I'd rather run through the house with scissors" are things you whisper to yourself, OK?

Snarky retorts are like a pressure-release valve: they lighten up your vibe. Just be careful who hears ya - we're not trying to start a fight or hurt someone's feelings on purpose. Do you *want* to? Probably. When we hurt, we want to hurt back. You have probably heard, "hurt people hurt people."

Be as kind as possible & set the 'toddler' aside...don't feed the animals. (podcast episode on "How to Deal with a Dumbass")

If this is a work thing, you've got to be careful how you respond. I know you want to knee-the-jerk, but that won't work. "OH, OK." See "REPORT 'EM" if it gets really bad, though.

POSTCARDS FOR THE PISSED-OFF

Go ahead and write some snarky cards. If you're mad, be mad for a little while. It's OK. It's not like you're claiming that as your personal identity.

Let it out to get it out and get on with it!

Postcards for the Pissed-off

Writing gets stuff out of your head and onto paper where you can deal with it.

So go ahead!
Write that card you'll never send.

It's you who will feel better in the end.

Go ahead and be a smart ass once in a while. The world won't stop turning.

Hey _____ , (you pick what you want to call this person)

I have _____ .
✓ had enough. __ to avoid you so I'm writing, instead.
__ installed security cameras so don't knock, ever.

I __
__ had hoped you'd figure
✓ can't wait to tell you
that you are _____
__ free __ welcome ✓ encouraged
to _____ .   __ F off.
__ embrace the Fleetwood Mac song "Go your own way." ✓ find someone else to annoy, thanks.

I hope you ___ .   ✓ make it.
__ have a great rest of your day.

Sorry/Not sorry,

(your name here, or not)

Write it out to get it out

What would be the most fun, next?
All those adventures mentioned earlier came as the answer to that one question. Asking "How can I have more fun today than I ever thought possible?" sets the ball in motion; answers come your way. And why not? In spite of the challenging content here, it is meant to clear space so you can go have a good time.

◆ ◆ ◆

Being impartial is the name of the game. Finding your funny bone will take you there. *Laughter is the lifter.* It will take you to even better places and man, it's contagious.

How many times have you gone out into the world with a smile on your dial? Total strangers smile back, don't they? Go light it up at the grocery store. Just waltzing through with your twinkle-toe'd self is helpful. You become a human tuning fork, casting silent notes of joy out to the world. It's only ever a good thing to be, do, feel and share those good vibrations.

Being productive will make you feel good, too. What nags at you to be accomplished? I have clients who "can't not do it" - they have to get their book written if only to leave a legacy for their family. Or, they feel pushed/pulled to share their story of healing as part of their own healing.

Tibor Spitz, a 90-something Holocaust survivor, blew me away with his sense of humor and love for everyone. He was like human pixie dust. What a gift to give others! What would be your idea of a good time? Service to others is more fulfilling than service to self. What's your gift and who is meant to receive it? When would now be a good time to move on with that 'calling' of yours? Just sayin'~

Raise your vibe and attract a new tribe. It's time to link arms, circle the wagons and have each other's back for real.

My biggest wish for you is that you know who truly has your back, not some fake-ass crap that weasels its way into your world with a smile, peddling absolute bullshit your way. Only you can stop them from further entry into your world, so do it for your own sanity.

So far, you've seen and heard a lot about who to look out for and how to deal with them.

You've learned how to see the writing on the wall and figure out trouble before it becomes your problem.

The list of free stuff ("Cheaper than Therapy" playlist) has things you can do to stay 'high' works *if you try it.*

And the hard lessons shared here can help you so much *if you apply them.*

It goes without saying that *if you allow dumbasses to run roughshod over your life now,* it won't get any better, later.

When times of stress happen, we resort to our lowest level of training. That said, UP your game now, please. Prepare yourself with the standards of care and the words that help you draw the line. **You want people who truly have your back, not take advantage of it.**

Please share this book with others you know who are struggling to kick some cans to the curb. Please. We have got to be stand-up guys for ourselves and show others how to do it in their own lives. It can be scary to put your foot down.

Just remember that's easier to seem a bit rude than to live with a lifetime of regret.

STRATEGY #4

REPORT 'EM

sometimes, if you want to see change for the better

you have to take things into your own hands

\- Clint Eastwood

It isn't easy to be the one who sticks up their hand first to say 'Ahem, but something is terribly wrong here." But *someone* has to open the dance floor. Reporting a dumbass sometimes becomes necessary. Calling in 'higher authorities' may be what you need to do to resolve the interference.

don't be scared

BE PREPARED

Plan ahead:

Decide where "the line" is!

Say what "the line" is!

Stick to your guns when they cross "the line" next time!!

Report 'em

- **SAY SOMETHING!!!**

- **File a report with your employer, landlord or other professional assistants.**

- **Reporting like this can really come in handy to evict or remove a dumbass from your world. In fact, it can save your life.**

My 62 y.o. female friend works in retail and is **sick of thieves!**

While shopping at a nearby store, she noticed a girl stealing.

From the privacy of two rows over she yelled...I mean YELLED:

"Hey, that girl on Aisle 6 is stealing!!" The girl dropped her stash and hit the door.

"I'm sick of it! WE end up having to pay for this so I'm saying something from now on. Enough already!"

Bravo!!

—•—

We all need to speak out against obvious wrongs or it appears that we are OK with it.

One of the ways we can look out for each other is to give a damn, first. Recently, an 80 year old man was attacked by a gang of 40 people. NO ONE STOPPED TO HELP HIM. What if that was your dad? How would you feel knowing people drove past and did nothing? Ouch. We gotta link arms and make a chain of strength - "it takes a village" is not just for young children.

When you are assessing a person or situation, make sure you notice who the "stand up guys" are and who they are *not*. Cowards cower. The question is: where do *you* stand?

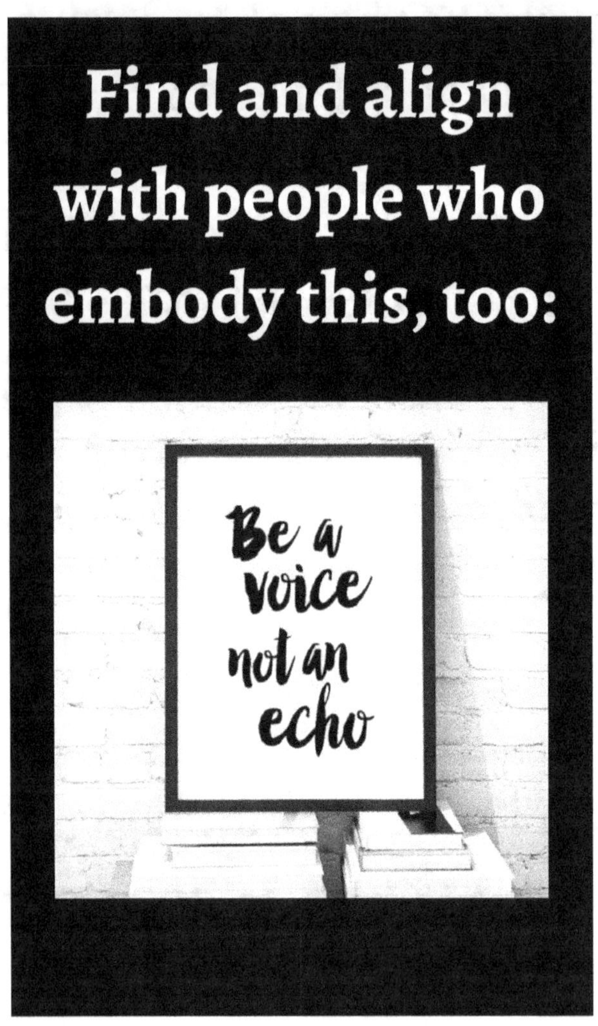

STRATEGY #5

EXIT:

*How and when to
evacuate the theater.*

Exit

- Excuse yourself - or them.
- You don't need an excuse.
- Close the gates and don't give 'em the pass code to get back in.
- Seems obvious but when was the last time you told a dumbass to get out?

MYTH: Everyone deserves another chance, and then another one and another one - we can't give up on people, right?

THE TRUTH: Sometimes, it's just their pattern - for life. It is, therefore (obviously) a lifetime pattern.

THE FIX: Decide how many chances you want to give away before you decide to compassionately lace up your walking shoes. Ahem.

Take a seat wherever you like but if you see the 'theater' is on fire, the exit row is ideal: it could burst into flames any second now and you want to have an exit strategy. In fact, the whole point of this book is to help you make wiser choices before it's too late. Tough love now is better than living with regret later, trust me.

Positioning yourself mentally is like game-face: you are prepared to up-and-leave if need be. The compassionate exit is pretty easy: *OH, OK, it's like that, huh? Well, I reckon I'll be going now.*

Excusing *them* from your world gets trickier. This is why it's best not to let 'em in the door but in case you have, don't worry - just decide they gotta go and set a deadline for their departure. Imagine the relief and peace!

If nothing changes, nothing changes. Change seats, so to speak. Find a balcony row or maybe just bag the show altogether. It's OK. **You may have 'bought a ticket' but that does not obligate you to be there through the encore.**

The young soul / old soul comparison ought to be enough for you to go on. Not everyone here is doing advanced math *and* it's true that all of us started out counting fingers.

If you struggle with change, it's time to get over it, honey bunny. Watch the Paloma Faith video (link next page) and realize change is going to happen. Will you be proactive or pushed into it?

Take the damn BULL by the horns. Toro!!!

OH, OK!

see the obvious?

You wouldn't ask a child to do geometry just because there are numbers on his blocks.

See who you're working with, what they're working with, *then* decide if it's going to work out.

It might be better if you walk away and let the kids play with their blocks, huh?

sometimes,
there is
nothing
left to do
but
move on

Sigma ft Paloma Faith - Changing (Official Video)

"Changing"
I don't understand playing by the same hand
How you find something new
I can't work it out what it's all about
I won't live my life through you

This ain't real, this ain't true
This ain't what I signed up to
This ain't right, it's no good
No good, oh

Everything is changing
And I've been here for too long
Going through the same things
I've been hurting too long,
Got to move on

5 RULES FOR THE ROAD AHEAD

Show & Tell

- *Take your time* previewing a new person - what is the "trailer ad" you are being shown? Be careful with "dramedies" because the funny bits may only be upfront...

- *Believe it* when they tell you who they are indeed, but also look at what they do...

- *Don't* place your heart, home, health or hope in the hands of just anyone...

- *Ask yourself IF* they qualify to be on your team & WHY...

- If your gut says NO, THAT IS ENOUGH TO GO ON, *literally.*

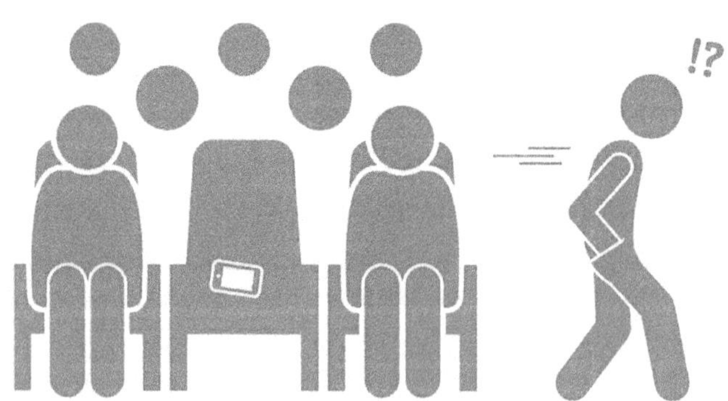

"I Don't Know" is the Beginning of New Possibilities.

Often the way we figure out what we want is by 'trial and error' - discovering that maybc it's a 'meh' instead of a 'wow.' There's huge value in this type of clarity! Knowing what you don't want is just as important as knowing what you *do* want.

The mother of all goals:

To be happy for no apparent reason

and in spite of present circumstances

RAISING YOUR FUN QUOTIENT

THE BEST QUESTION YOU COULD EVER ASK:

"How can I have more fun today than I ever thought possible?"

This question produces results without any effort on your part.
Just ask, then forget about it. Your day will improve, promise!

Knowing what to look for is half the battle.

If you see yourself in these pages, then buck up and become a stand-up guy for yourself, your family and your future. This book was written to make you laugh at some really hard facts.

"Stay away from negative people. They have a problem for every solution."

- Albert Einstein

◆ ◆ ◆

Don't shoot the messenger. Just get busy raising your expertise in dealing with DUH, managing the would-be actions of others by excusing them from the party.

The best way to win a fight is to not be in one.

THE FORMULA FOR CHANGE:

Awareness + Acceptance + Action = Change

"Acceptance" is the

to peace.

What 'is' is what shows up.
It is what it is & it is what it ain't.

Finding 'observer mode' keeps
you light, not carrying a load.

Rubber Hitting the Road

When you walk in to deal with a dumbass you have to know what you want out of it - rehearse your spiel. Get it into your head now, before emotions flare.

It can be hard to remain neutral, untriggered, 'still like water,' but the reward for doing it is worth the effort. "OH, OK!" gets that ball rolling. It becomes the perfect response to keep yourself in neutral gear. So much depends on how you say it, too. You can be sarcastic, and may feel like they deserve a swift verbal kick, but does that serve you best? "OH, OK" can be said without being inflammatory. It then becomes a statement of acceptance, as in "OH, OK, it's like that? Oh, OK." Or, just say it to yourself.

What about you?

Are you called to help others? As you know, you can't 'give it' if you don't 'own it' or have it to give. That said, the right frame of mind, sans cymbal-clanging monkeys, is what you are aiming for now.

Do you believe you can make positive changes in your life? I know it seems like a huge task but it is worth the effort. You will free yourself from sources of anxiety, discouragement and drama.

This analogy might help put perspective on the task: imagine that you want to organize the hall closet. It's jam-packed with stuff. You know you need to deal with it or it will keep falling out when you open the closet door. "Awareness" is always the first step in evolution.

That 'stuff' was manifested by you or someone in your world, right? This fact alone indicates you know how to bring things you want or need into your world.

If you want to get that closet organized, you will likely pull everything out, first. Now, it's an even bigger mess than when you started. This is part of the process and cannot be avoided. It's just "stuff" right?

"Acceptance" is the key to peace. You know where you are headed: a more organized closet. In spite of the mess, you know it will get better.

Taking action: you may want to inventory what you have on-hand. You may realize there are things you no longer need. "OH, OK." Remove them and voila, you have more space for the stuff you want to keep.

You might need some bins to organize your stuff. Do you want clear bins or would you rather not see inside, opting for an external label, instead? What type of organizational tools will you need? Is it shelving? Baskets? Repurposing of shoe boxes, perhaps? It all depends on what you want, or need, next. It might simply be a visual preference or a very logical choice, irrespective of looks.

Systematically, you place back only the things you want to keep. *Wow, that feels better, doesn't it?* It looks so much better. When you open the hallway closet door next time, nothing comes tumbling out at you. YOU feel better. Whew. Mental fung shui, if you will.

The same is true about 'inventorying' the influences in your life. Are they helpful to your frame of mind? Keep those 'sources' around. If not, excuse yourself, or them, from the 'table.' This book highlighted a few of the ways you can do this.

Proactive steps you can take now will make all the difference tomorrow. Turn to other channels for news, for instance. Now that you know the script readers are not really delivering the full picture, seek full disclosure from those with a reputation for investigative journalism. At least you aren't listening to half-truths any longer. What a relief.

Once you check out the other platforms for real news, it's going to be hard on you. I know this already. A 'deer in the headlights' effect, this reality-check is nothing short of shocking. But to stay in the dark is to be overruled and suffer a loss of freedom you currently enjoy.

It is easier to keep your freedom than to try and get it back from those who happily steal it away. Pay close attention to what is happening and get proactive in the battle for both our freedom, and our souls.

The whole world isn't your responsibility. Only your world is your job. Handle it with awareness of what is, and take action so you don't feel like a sitting duck.

Build up your 'team' of influencers, beginning with those who bring light, joy and positivity to the table. By raising your vibe you attract a new tribe.

Listen to your own inner GPS and trust the hunches. You will be guided where *your* soul is happiest. If you are called to it there is a way to do it.

Ask for signs and trust what you see/hear/feel. That 'still small voice' whispers truths all the time. LISTEN.

Armed with skills, reading the signs,
Trusting your 'Spidey Sense,' one step at a time
One thing you know, that's for sure,
Your footing's more solid than ever before.

Taking a step further today than yesterday, you move in the direction you are called: your "BIG Yes!" You have already seen how 'crazy ideas' work out; that you probably won't die from trying. Becoming a clear, intentional creator is your true nature!

158

BECOME THE AUTHORITY IN YOUR LIFE

It isn't selfish…
it is essential.

LISTEN TO YOUR "BIG YES!"

If there are elements of a "no," sit tight because somethin' ain't right. Trust that much. Ask for a sign to confirm and affirm your hunch. It will come. If isn't what you wanted to hear, listen anyway.

Consult the playlist when you feel blues hanging around too long. Strive to stay "high" and above the fray.

Notice all you have manifested so far and remember, you're just getting started. Imagine how much more you can do without the distractions of a dumbass in your life! Imagine the benefits of hearing clearly, without the cymbal-clanging monkeys, what your inner GPS is telling you to do next!

Don't buy into the hype and boogey-man attempts to create fear. Just laugh. They are knuckle-dragging, first-rung of the ladder, itty bitty small-minded toddlers, shaking their rattles, after all. Do something to silence them. Be proactive instead of reactive. Your good judgment skills will manifest the peace you've been wanting all along.

And finally, once you do a proverbial pat on the toddler's head, make sure you lock the playpen gate behind you.

Not everyone belongs in a foxhole with you, Honey Child. And that's OK, too. 'Pick-and-flick' well for yourself. heheh

More like, *Ohh, OK!*

If you found this book helpful, *say* it forward! Please leave a positive review on Amazon telling folks what stood out for you. Maybe it was just refreshing to finally have someone take the *bull-honky* by the horns, eh? Now it's your turn...

Thank you *so* very much!

https://amzn.to/3FLO51D

ABOUT THE AUTHOR

Two-Time #1 International Best Selling Author, Lonnee Rey

Other books:
"Life lessons learned from a lousy mother"
"Wake Up Winning" (one chapter)

Podcasts:
"How to Deal with a Dumbass (a spiritual perspective)"
"Mid-life My Ass, I'm just getting started!"
"Bold Movers & Shakers: stories that rock the boat"
"Cougar Talk Radio: the comedy show for anyone who has ever been single"